The Pleasure in/of the Text

European Connections

Studies in Comparative Literature,
Intermediality and Aesthetics

Volume 43

edited by
Hugues Azérad and Marion Schmid

PETER LANG

Oxford • Bern • Berlin • Bruxelles • New York • Wien

Fabien Arribert-Narce,
Fuhito Endo and Kamila
Pawlikowska (eds)

The Pleasure in/of the Text

About the Joys and Perversities of Reading

PETER LANG

Oxford • Bern • Berlin • Bruxelles • New York • Wien

Bibliographic information published by Die Deutsche Nationalbibliothek.
Die Deutsche Nationalbibliothek lists this publication in the Deutsche
Nationalbibliografie; detailed bibliographic data is available on the
Internet at http://dnb.d-nb.de.

A catalogue record for this book is available from the British Library.

Library of Congress Cataloging-in-Publication Data

Names: Arribert-Narce, Fabien, editor. | Endō, Fuhito, 1961- editor. |
  Pawlikowska, Kamila, editor.
Title: The pleasure in/of the text : about the joys and perversities of
  reading / [edited by] Fabien Arribert-Narce, Endo Fuhito, Kamila
  Pawlikowska.
Description: Oxford ; New York : Peter Lang, [2021] | Series: European
  connections : studies in comparative literature, intermediality and
  aesthetics, 1424-3792 ; volume 43 | Includes bibliographical references
  and index.
Identifiers: LCCN 2020057122 (print) | LCCN 2020057123 (ebook) |
  ISBN 9781789977004 (paperback) | ISBN 9781789977264 (ebook) |
  ISBN 9781789977271 (epub)
Subjects: LCSH: Barthes, Roland--Criticism and interpretation. |
  Literature--Aesthetics. | Reading--Philosophy.
Classification: LCC P85.B33 P58 2021 (print) | LCC P85.B33 (ebook) | DDC
  801--dc23
LC record available at https://lccn.loc.gov/2020057122
LC ebook record available at https://lccn.loc.gov/2020057123

Cover image: Matthias Stom (1615–1659), *A Young Man Reading at Candlelight*.
Oil on canvas. In the public domain.

Cover design by Peter Lang Ltd.

ISSN 1424-3792
ISBN 978-1-78997-700-4 (print)
ISBN 978-1-78997-726-4 (ePDF)
ISBN 978-1-78997-727-1 (ePub)

© Peter Lang Group AG 2021

Published by Peter Lang Ltd, International Academic Publishers,
52 St Giles, Oxford, OX1 3LU, United Kingdom
oxford@peterlang.com, www.peterlang.com

Fabien Arribert-Narce, Fuhito Endo and Kamila Pawlikowska have asserted
their right under the Copyright, Designs and Patents Act, 1988, to be identified
as Editors of this Work.

This publication has been peer reviewed.

Contents

FABIEN ARRIBERT-NARCE, FUHITO ENDO AND
KAMILA PAWLIKOWSKA

Introduction   1

PART I   Perversity, Madness and Projective Reading, at the
            Margins of the Text: Image and Paratext in Barthes   13

ALEX WATSON

1 The Perverse Footnote: Roland Barthes's *The Pleasure of the
Text* (1973) and the Politics of Paratextuality   15

PATRICK FFRENCH

2 *To Enter Madly into the Image*: Reading Projectively in Barthes   37

PART II   On Pleasure, Fatigue and Death in/of the
            Text: Textual Exhaustion and Oscillations   59

KOHEI KUWADA

3 Pleasure and Fatigue of the Barthesian Text   61

FUHITO ENDO

4 Genealogy of Textual Necrophilia or Death Drive: Barthes,
Freud, De Man and Mehlman   67

KRISTA BONELLO RUTTER GIAPPONE

5 Tragicomic Pleasure and Tickling-Teasing Oscillation in John
Marston's *Antonio* Plays   83

PART III   Barthes and Japan, the 'Empire of Signs': *Signifiance*
            and Undialectical Writing   105

FABIEN ARRIBERT-NARCE

6 Taking Signs for What They Are: Roland Barthes, Chris
Marker and the Pleasure of *Texte Japon*   107

ANDY STAFFORD

7 The Barthesian 'Double Grasp' in Japan: Reading as
Undialectical Writing   129

Bibliography   153

Notes on Contributors   159

Index   163

FABIEN ARRIBERT-NARCE, FUHITO ENDO AND
KAMILA PAWLIKOWSKA

Introduction

Reading is a peculiar kind of experience. Although its practice and theory have a very long tradition, the question of aesthetic pleasure is as perplexing as ever. Why do we read? What exactly thrills us in the text? When it comes to the pleasure of reading, authors often feel entitled to instruct readers as well as other writers. Aristotle maintained that, in its capacity to excite and purge dangerous emotions, art can be therapeutic. Shakespeare sought both to entertain and instruct, while Coleridge proposed 'suspension of disbelief' as a condition of readerly enjoyment. Sterne seduced his readers with digressions and figurative meanings, while Rousseau directly spoke of solitary readers whose 'reading with one hand only' invited analogies between the physical body and the body of the text. In the nineteenth century, many novelists used imagination, material detail and writerly craft to achieve 'solidity of specification', resulting in vivid, 'believable' pictures. Many at that time searched for moral edification and 'truth', while others denied that these can be pleasurable. Oscar Wilde addressed the allegedly universal desire for truth and insisted that creative writing ('lying') can be a source of delight to both writers and readers. Russian formalists rejected the pleasures of 'visualisation' altogether and suggested that reading strange descriptions of familiar objects would pleasantly stimulate readers' senses as they guess and rediscover them anew. According to Natsume Sōseki, readerly pleasure is generated by trimming down the descriptions to striking essentials, by reducing them to what he called 'sweet fire'. Sartre, on the other hand, argued that the pleasure of the text cannot be felt directly but must be hidden; the readers, he claimed, 'must be solicited by the charm that they do not see'. Drawing on the pleasure-pain binary, Adam Phillips introduced the notion of a 'tickling narrative'. According to him, the readers delight in blurred points characteristic of this kind of narrative: they are able to experience an intensely anguished (and pleasurable) confusion 'because the tickling narrative, unlike the sexual narrative, has no climax'. Instead of taking a 'close-reading' approach, Susan Sontag drew attention to the political context of the reader. She noted that reading is circumstantial and may have a liberating and transvaluing effect, as well as reactionary and stifling.

One of the most prominent scholars having addressed this issue in the twentieth century is undeniably Roland Barthes, who distinguished between the 'ordinary' pleasure of reading and bliss (*jouissance*), a delight so profound that it cannot be expressed in words. About fifty years after the publication of seminal essays such as *Empire of Signs* (1970) and *The Pleasure of the Text* (1973), that we would like to revisit in this volume, the long-lasting influence of his theories on readerly pleasure is still evident today in academia and beyond. This is reflected, for example, by the widespread use of some of the neologisms he coined in his post-structuralist works of the 1960s and 1970s, such as the distinction between *studium* and *punctum* in *Camera Lucida* (1980).[1] More specifically, given its broadranging interdisciplinary grid of analysis encompassing formal and stylistic issues but also socio-historical, political and ideological aspects, the Barthesian transversal approach to the notion of 'text' has produced a range of critical tools which are still pertinent to evaluate the new ways and modalities of reading in the digital age, that some have called an 'age of

---

1   See Roland Barthes, *Camera Lucida: Reflections on Photography* (1980), trans. by Richard Howard (New York: Hill and Wang, 1981), pp. 25–8. Barthes defines *studium* as 'a kind of general, [human] interest', 'an average affect', which 'has the extension of a field', and 'which I perceive quite familiarly as a consequence of my knowledge, my culture'; 'it always refers to a classical body of information' (*Camera Lucida*, pp. 25–6). On the other hand, *punctum* is of an emotional nature and 'will break (or punctuate) the *studium*'; 'It is this element which rises from the scene, shoots out of it like an arrow, and pierces me' (*ibid.*, p. 26).

distraction' dominated by screens and images.[2] Also intermedial by nature and concerned with the interrelations between various art forms (paintings, photos, films, music and textual productions) and their reception,[3] Barthes's reflection on readerly pleasure oscillates between critical theory and a phenomenology of writing/reading, sensitive to the materiality of the artworks considered and to the emotional dimension of the readers' response. For him, there is in fact a fundamental ambiguity attached to this notion from this perspective: '"pleasure" here […] sometimes extends to bliss, sometimes is opposed to it. […] I need to distinguish euphoria, fulfillment, comfort (the feeling of repletion when culture penetrates freely), from shock, disturbance, even loss, which are proper to ecstasy, to bliss.'[4] 'Pleasure' therefore tends to resist our attempts to define it in this context, and to provide a systematic analysis: 'No "thesis" on the pleasure of the text is possible; […] And yet, against and in spite of everything, the text gives me bliss' (p. 34). To solve this conundrum, Barthes made a conceptual distinction between what he calls '*texte scriptible*' ('writerly', bliss-giving text, which has a power of disruption) and '*texte lisible*' ('readerly' text),[5] which provides a cultural, civilised 'pleasure', and is 'linked to a comfortable practice of reading' (p. 14). Whereas the latter, that is, the text of pleasure, 'contents, fills, grants euphoria' and conforms to social and literary conventions, the text of bliss 'imposes a state of loss' and 'unsettles the reader's historical, cultural, psychological assumptions, the consistency of his tastes, values, memories, brings to a crisis his relation with language' (p. 14). Barthes argues that in 'texts of pleasure', *writing* is understood as a transitive verb that requires a direct object. These texts refer to something

---

2   See Alan Jacobs, *The Pleasures of Reading in an Age of Distraction* (New York: Oxford University Press, 2011). See also Christopher Butler, *Pleasure and the Arts: Enjoying Literature, Painting, and Music* (Oxford: Oxford University Press, 2005).

3   See Roland Barthes's collection of essays *Image-Music-Text*, selected and trans. by Stephen Heath (New York: Hill and Wang, 1977).

4   Roland Barthes, *The Pleasure of the Text* (1973), trans. by Richard Miller (New York: Hill and Wang, 1975), p. 19.

5   See Roland Barthes, *S/Z* (1970), trans. by Richard Miller (New York: Hill and Wang, 1974), pp. 3–16. The distinction between 'readerly' and 'writerly' texts in *S/Z* prefigures the distinction between texts of 'pleasure' and 'bliss' in *The Pleasure of the Text*, and between '*studium*' and '*punctum*' in *Camera Lucida*.

beyond themselves in an attempt at representing reality – in this sense, there is pleasure *in* the text, that is, in the story or plot, in the characters and places represented, stemming from various forms of projected reality and a fluctuating degree of adequation between the text and what it refers to. This is potentially a refuge for escapist readings, but also for realism and narrative or *romanesque* pleasure. On the other hand, 'texts of bliss' always have a self-referential dimension according to Barthes, whatever they explicitly refer to. Being linked on a formal level with the pleasure of the metatext, but also with a certain sense of aesthetic hermeticism, they require an active role of the reader, effectively activating chains of signifiers to unlock potential meanings and enjoy the 'layering of significance (*signifiance*)' (p. 12) – which is defined as follows in *The Pleasure of the Text*: 'What is significance? It is meaning, *insofar as it is sensually produced*' (p. 61). From a Barthesian perspective, *jouissance* in the act of reading therefore implies an involvement of the whole (desiring) body of the reader, and multifold interactions with the (erotic) body of the text – or in other words, the text *as* body, if we follow this metaphor: 'The text you write must prove to me *that it desires me*. This proof exists: it is writing. Writing is: the science of the various blisses of language, its Kama Sutra (this science has but one treatise: writing itself)' (p. 6).[6] Barthes emphasises the complexity of this reception process, which is far from linear or unidimensional:

> this body of bliss is also *my historical subject*; for it is at the conclusion of a very complex process of biographical, historical, sociological, neurotic elements (education, social class, childhood configuration, etc.) that I control the contradictory interplay of (cultural) pleasure and (non-cultural) bliss […]: anachronic subject, adrift. (pp. 62–3)

Ruptures, disruptions (of language) and (self-)contradictions can be a source of bliss for Barthes, who even suggests that joy and perversion are inextricably linked in the process of reading – and writing – a text, with an interplay of erotic and masochistic impulses. If the potential danger of reading is a well-known topos in the history of literature, with several great

6   Barthes adds that 'The pleasure of the text is that moment when my body pursues its own ideas – for my body does not have the same ideas I do' (*The Pleasure of the Text*, p. 17).

classic novels such as Cervantes' *Don Quixote* and Flaubert's *Madame Bovary* showing their eponymous characters overwhelmed by the books they read and unable to distinguish fiction from reality, Barthes argues that the pleasures and perversities of the text should be addressed concomitantly given their structural interdependence and multiple practical and theoretical entanglements. In this respect, his aesthetic and ethical approach to reading/writing (and to pleasure) is based on the Proustian notion of *intermittence*:[7]

> Is not the most erotic portion of a body *where the garment gapes*? In perversion (which is the realm of textual pleasure) there are no 'erogenous zones' […]; it is intermittence, as psychoanalysis has so rightly stated, which is erotic: the intermittence of skin flashing between two articles of clothing (trousers and sweater), between two edges (the open-necked shirt, the glove and the sleeve); it is this flash itself which seduces, or rather: the staging of an appearance-as-disappearance. (pp. 9–10)

This dynamic process of reading is made of holes and gaps, interruptions and fragmentation, the emotional investment of the *punctum* puncturing the *studium* surface of the text – these two elements 'composing' as Jacques Derrida put it, and therefore needing each other.[8] Beyond the artificial separation of form and content, this is how the 'plurality' of the text can be revealed,[9] and its 'flesh' or *signifiance* fully appreciated.

Taking the work of Barthes as a central reference, and in a dialogue with the various approaches described above, the aim of this collection of essays is to investigate a variety of themes and issues associated with the question of readerly pleasure or, more precisely, of pleasure 'in' and 'of' the text. What conditions should be fulfilled to satisfy readerly expectations? How do specific ways of reading – psychoanalytic, feminist, post-colonial,

---

7 See Marcel Proust, 'The Intermittences of the Heart', in *In Search of Lost Time*, ed. by Christopher Prendergast, *Sodom and Gomorrah II*, trans. by John Sturrock (New York: Viking, 2004), pp. 150–66; Thomas Baldwin, 'Chapter 2: Eros, Rhythm', in *Roland Barthes: The Proust Variations* (Liverpool: Liverpool University Press, 2019), pp. 47–77.

8 Jacques Derrida, 'Les Morts de Roland Barthes', *Poétique*, n°47 (1981), pp. 269–92 (p. 274).

9 Barthes, *S/Z*, p. 4.

etc. – approach the problem of the pleasure of the text, and in what ways do these specialised readings, especially those which seek to uncover the 'latent content', such as Marxist, Freudian or Lacanian, help us understand our aesthetic pleasures? How can style be a source of readers' enjoyment? How do literary and ideological pleasures intersect? What satisfaction can be derived from 'historicised' and a-historical reading? How do writers organise texts to maximise their effects? What is exhibited and what is relegated to the peripheries of the text (e.g. to footnotes)? To what extent do the margins of the text, or paratext, influence our ways of reading? How do intermedial configurations combining different art forms such as images and texts affect the transmission of pleasure? These are some of the questions that will be addressed in this volume.

Some of the chapters gathered in this book might tempt us to speculate on what could be described as an aesthetic genealogy, wherein a Barthesian pleasure of the text can enjoy intertextual dialogues with a set of preceding literary discourses. One of them may be Flaubert's aspiration of writing 'a book for nothing' and its privileging of the style of the text for its own sake. Mallarmé and his poetic language can be immediately associated with this textual self-referential aesthetics; his symbolist urge to create a pure poetics without any referent is, significantly, reminiscent of Barthesian writing as an intransitive act as well. This kind of literary self-referentiality – or rather non-referentiality – moreover, reminds us of Oscar Wilde's 'language-for-language's-sake' criticism; in this connection, his interest in French symbolist poets assumes a fresh significance. It is indeed very easy to reduce this type of literary attitude to a typically escapist and aestheticist ideology, but at the same time we need to pay careful attention to the ways in which such textuality is not necessarily contradictory of its potentially emancipating politics, one of whose examples is Wilde's socialism. It is worth remembering that William Morris' aesthetic socialism worked as a strong and decisive inspiration for both Wilde's politics and aesthetics.[10]

---

10   Concerning the potential socialist politics of Wilde's aesthetics of textual non-referentiality and its connections with Morris and French symbolism, see Fuhito Endo, 'Modernism as Anti-Modernity: Oscar Wilde and His Negative Materialism', *Oscar Wilde Studies*, n°19 (2020), pp. 43–56.

Given these literary and historical associations, therefore, we may feel emboldened to contextualise Barthes's 'writing degree zero' within such an aesthetic and political genealogy, whilst simultaneously reexamining his mentions of Mallarmé, Flaubert, Blanchot or Rimbaud as representative of 'writing and silence'.[11] It goes without saying that *Writing Degree Zero* is a suggestive manifestation of the simultaneity and non-contradiction of Barthesian textual *jouissance* and his radical political views. Of particular interest are possible connections between his sensual enjoyment of the linguistic materiality of textual non-signification and his attempted reinterpretation of Marxist materialism in this vein. This genealogical evocation of semantic absence and its linguistic presence or materiality concurrently invokes what Michel Foucault terms 'the being of language' in *The Order of Things* (the original French title is *Les Mots et les Choses*), where we encounter a literature 'from the nineteenth century' which 'began to bring language back to light once more in its own being'. Foucault continues:

> For now we no longer have that primary, that absolutely initial, word upon which the infinite movement of discourse was founded and by which it was limited; henceforth, language was to grow with no point of departure, no end, and no promise. It is the traversal of this futile yet fundamental space that the text of literature traces from day to day.[12]

We are reminded of the Barthesian textual 'drifting (*dérive*)' and thereby led to reconsider his literary materialism in the context of Foucault's 'words and things'.

Noteworthy here is a sort of Heideggerian 'being' which manifests itself 'from Hölderlin to Mallarmé and on to Antonin Artaud' as something that 'achieved autonomous existence, and separated itself from all other language with a deep scission, only by forming a sort of "counter-discourse", and by finding its way back from the representative or signifying function of language to this raw being that had been forgotten since the sixteenth

---

11   Roland Barthes, *Writing Degree Zero* (1953), trans. by Annette Lavers and Colin Smith (New York: Hill and Wang, 2012), pp. 74–8.

12   Michel Foucault, *The Order of Things: An Archaeology of the Human Sciences* (1966), trans. by Alan Sheridan (New York and London: Routledge, 2002), p. 49.

century'.[13] Thus, 'this raw being' – or 'the living being of language' –[14] materialises itself in a totally different ontological form from 'the representative or signifying function of language', which allows us to say that literary language here reveals this 'being' materially while concealing it semantically. This paradox of a linguistic presence of semantic or representative absence is what inspires us to juxtapose Heidegger, Blanchot, Foucault and Barthes. Or rather, we are induced to re-politicise Barthesian textual materiality in the context of a set of endeavours to radicalise Heidegger's potentially dangerous and reactionary ontology of 'being', represented by Blanchot, Foucault, or even Derrida.

***

In the first part of the volume, entitled 'Perversity, Madness and Projective Reading, at the Margins of the Text', Alex Watson first examines the pleasure of annotations in Barthes's *The Pleasure of the Text*, a theme that – although the book itself only contains one footnote – not only enhances but also illuminates the textual practice of the author. Indeed, as Watson argues, a hitherto unacknowledged affinity exists between Barthes's key claims about textuality in *Pleasure* and the act of footnoting, which is confirmed by the paratextual structure of this work. Contradicting Gérard Genette's claim that 'the implicit creed and spontaneous ideology of the paratext' is always 'the authorial point of view',[15] the Barthesian position on footnotes and annotations tends to complicate or even undermine authorial authority. After a critical discussion of this singular position – in *Pleasure* and other works – in the main body of the chapter, Watson concludes his study by considering the relevance of Barthes's work on (para)textual pleasure today, showing the extent to which it continues – like footnotes – to interrupt us, speak beyond its immediate situation and elicit new insights.

13   *Ibid.*
14   *Ibid.*, p. 48.
15   Gérard Genette, *Paratexts: Thresholds of Interpretation*, trans. by Jane E. Lewin (Cambridge: Cambridge University Press, 2001), p. 408.

Patrick ffrench addresses this question from a different angle in his chapter of the book which explores, through close discussion of selected instances of Barthes's writing on the image, the motif of 'entering in', a projective and evaluative relation to the object which underpins a mode of reading in Barthes. It focuses in particular on an early 'report' on the new technology of Cinemascope, through which Barthes entertains the possibility (or the fantasy) of a participation on the 'stage of History', and, in a second instance, on the penultimate chapter of *Camera Lucida*, in which Barthes writes of his desire to 'enter, madly' into the image of Casanova's dance with the automaton Rosalba in Fellini's 1976 film *Casanova*. Close analyses of these examples are linked by an exploration of the *champ aveugle* (blind field) of the image, offering thereby a perspective on Barthes's relation to the cinema.

In the second part of the book, which also largely focuses on the Barthesian corpus and more specifically on the themes of textual exhaustion and oscillations, Kohei Kuwada first considers the dialectics between pleasure and fatigue in the work of the famous French semiologist. Taking as a starting point Barthes's concept of 'writing aloud', presented as an example of his 'aesthetics of textual pleasure' in the final section of *The Pleasure of the Text*, Kuwada proposes to listen carefully to the *sounds* Barthes's own body emits unwittingly when he talks aloud about pleasure. By doing so, he brings to light an inseparable and intricate connection between pleasure and fatigue in the writings and thought of the French writer, even if these two terms seem opposed at first glance. Barthes's 'fatigue', defined in *The Neutral* as 'the infinitude but livable in the body', is not only caused by the stereotypes and *doxa* that he so abhorred, but also by the endless, Sisyphean process of their deconstruction – that he desperately sought to escape in the 1970s. Kuwada argues that without taking into account and even sharing (as a reader) such fatigue, one cannot fully understand what Barthes meant by 'pleasure' in his work.

Fuhito Endo extends these reflections in the psychoanalytical field by offering in his study a genealogy of *textual necrophilia* (or lethality) in the work of Barthes, Freud, de Man and Mehlman. These authors examine the act of reading from different perspectives, but share an appreciation of it as a process that endures (and enjoys) contradictions and disruptions. Endo first shows the fundamental ambiguity that lies at the core of Barthes's analysis of textual bliss/pleasure by making a comparison with the Freudian approach to displeasure, which is 'beyond' but at the same time *within* pleasure. The discussion of this paradoxical, chiasmic simultaneity of opposed terms is then extended to Paul de Man's concept of 'allegory', whose deconstructive power has a lot in common with Barthes's 'text of bliss'. The chapter concludes with a reflection on the politics of textuality, via Jeffrey Mehlman's interpretation of textual *matter* in the work of Marx, which is compared with Barthes's notion of a 'pure materiality' of the text; as Endo puts it, they both 'reveal themselves in the midst of textual disconnection/ connection of semantic or discursive maximisation (absolute affirmation) and zero degree writing/reading (radical negation)'.

In her chapter focusing on tragicomic pleasure and tickling-teasing textual oscillations, Krista Bonello Rutter Giappone starts by challenging the critics who include the genre of tragicomedy within the tragic paradigm, discussing as a case in point Marston's *Antonio* plays. She claims that tragicomedy, as a mode in delicate balance between tragedy and comedy, neither one nor the other, yet drawing upon both, is the source of a unique pleasure springing from its double-edged character. In tragicomedy, the metatheatrical dimension may provide a margin for *play*, opening up the space for a potential of re-accentuation that could alter the balance between constituent genres. Bonello Rutter Giappone analyses the see-sawing movements at work in Marston's plays, written for a Renaissance boy company, where discrepancies and lack of contiguity between actor and role were at the (cracked) heart of the game; where the underlined artifice extended its play, and unashamedly proffered (semi-exposed) trickery, to the audience.

The third part of the volume continues the Barthesian journey through the paradoxes of textual pleasure by making a detour to Japan, that Barthes called in a famous essay the 'Empire of Signs'. In his chapter entitled 'Taking Signs for What They Are', Fabien Arribert-Narce focuses first on the pleasure that Barthes and French filmmaker Chris Marker derived from their reception of Japanese 'signs' in the 1960s and 1970s. He argues that in *Empire of Signs* (1970), Barthes tends to perceive and present Japan as a fragmented text whose signs he cannot fully understand. Likewise, in Marker's unclassifiable film *Sunless* (1982) and photo-text *Le Dépays* (*The Un-Country*, 1982), Japan appears as a succession of still and moving icons that trigger and at the same time resist interpretation (by Westerners). Barthes and Marker's encounter with this fascinating – and largely fantasised – Japanese 'text' prompted them to develop a reflection on the very readability of signs, taking into account their concrete, visual dimension. 'Exempted of *meaning*' and irreducible to a set of fixed signifi-cations from the perspective of Western readers, Japanese signs are praised for their 'fleshiness' and *signifiance* (i.e. 'meaning, *insofar as it is sensually produced*' according to Barthes),[16] which becomes the basis of a singular ethics, aesthetics and eventually erotics of seeing/reading – but also writing and filming – guided by a search for pleasure.

Also considering in his study Barthes's 'reading' of Japan, Andy Stafford concentrates in his chapter on the author's writing strategies, primarily through his work on Jules Michelet, but also the 'double grasp' that he uses in *Empire of Signs*. The 'double grasp' that Barthes finds in Michelet's historiography is then applied to 'reading' and 'writing' Japan. Stafford argues that Barthes's 'pleasure' is to write 'undialectically'; however, the 'undialectical' is not understood in this context as anti-dialectical or a-dialectical. It is rather the pleasure of writing open-endedly, a 'two-term' dialectic as Barthes calls it – that is, without any synthesis.

With Barthes, and beyond Barthes, *The Pleasure in/of the Text* volume will address the question of readerly and aesthetic pleasure from multiple angles, following an interdisciplinary approach that will explore both theor-etical and practical aspects. We do hope that our readers will find pleasure in reading this book!

16   Barthes, *The Pleasure of the Text*, p. 61.

PART I

Perversity, Madness and Projective Reading, at the Margins of the Text

Image and Paratext in Barthes

ALEX WATSON

1 The Perverse Footnote

Roland Barthes's *The Pleasure of the Text* (1973) and the Politics of Paratextuality

Introduction: Of Refrigeration and Interruption

In a sub-essay entitled 'Of textual notes' in his famous 'Preface' to his exhaustive edition of *The Plays of William Shakespeare* (1785), the English biographer, editor, lexicographer, literary critic and poet Samuel Johnson asserts that:

> The mind is refrigerated by interruption; the thoughts are diverted from the principle subject; the reader is weary, he suspects not why; and at last throws away the book, which he has too diligently studied.[1]

Johnson is explaining why he endeavoured to make frugal use of annotation in his edition. As this comment shows, like many editors in the eighteenth century, and indeed many editors, writers and readers today, Johnson envisions annotation as an intrusion, sometimes necessary but always to some degree unwelcome. What is most striking, however, is his metaphor of 'refrigeration'. Surely, to freeze, we might insist, is the more disruptive act, since it involves exposing an object suddenly to a colder temperature, whereas to refrigerate implies keeping it in a cold place for a long time – without interruption? Furthermore, we might consider being interrupted as we carry out an absorbing task an irritation that makes our

[1]   Samuel Johnson, 'Of Textual Notes', 'Preface to Shakespeare', *The Yale Edition of the Works of Samuel Johnson*, ed. by Arthur Sherbo (New York: Yale University Press, 1968), vol. 7, pp. 59–113 (p. 111).

temper more heated; for Johnson, on the contrary, interruption cools the mind, nullifying consciousness, leading to exhaustion and eventually abandonment.

In contrast to Johnson's conception of interruption as imposition, in *The Pleasure of the Text* (1973) Roland Barthes envisions interruption as a catalyst to epiphany. In Barthes's view, the pleasure of the text resides primarily in those moments of second-order reading when we are thrown outside the text and into contemplative activity: 'it produces, in me, the best pleasure if it manages to make itself heard indirectly; if, reading it, I am led to look up often, to listen to something else'.[2] For Barthes, the fractured consciousness occasioned by interruption is a more fertile one, enabling us to circumvent our customary modes of thought, and receive new insights. While Barthes would dispute Johnson's portrayal of interruption as interference, he might, however, agree with him on its infrigidating effect. In Barthes's view, the most profound pleasure reading can produce in us is what he refers to elsewhere as '*satori*', a term he derives from Zen Buddhism, and which he defines in his idiosyncratic analysis of Japanese culture *Empire of Signs* (1970; Eng. trans.) as 'the blank which erases in us the reign of the Codes, the breach of that internal recitation which constitutes our person'.[3] While Johnson and Barthes are divided on many issues, they are both united in envisaging interruption as an occasion in which we empty out ourselves, leading for Johnson to ennui, for Barthes to a form of enlightenment.

Why does it matter that two writings separated by different languages and almost 200 years possess such similarities and differences? Well, as an early example of eighteenth-century Bardolatry, Johnson's 'Preface' was an important document in establishing not only Shakespeare's reputation as perhaps literature's greatest genius, but also in promoting what Michel Foucault famously labelled 'the author function' –[4] the idea that the writer

2   Roland Barthes, *The Pleasure of the Text*, trans. by Richard Miller (New York: Hill and Wang, 1975), p. 24. All references hereafter given in parentheses in the text.

3   Roland Barthes, *Empire of Signs* (1970), trans. by Richard Howard (New York: Hill and Wang, 1983), p. 75.

4   Michel Foucault, 'What Is an Author?', in *Modern Criticism and Theory: A Reader*, ed. by David Lodge (London: Longman, 1988), pp. 197–210 (p. 204).

of a literary work should be viewed as its sole originator – as the central locus of literary interpretation and the crucial determinant in literary copyright from the eighteenth century until the present. And Johnson's own celebrity, enshrined in James Boswell's *Life of Samuel Johnson* (1791), did much to seal the dominance of this concept. Moreover, in creating his famous *A Dictionary of the English Language* (1755) and in his editing and biographical writings about other earlier writers, Johnson also played a crucial role in constructing an 'official' version of the English language and an authorised account of English literature. Johnson might therefore be said to promote those very literary values – of the writer as *author* (or sole originary genius) rather than *scriptor* (or blender of pre-existing texts); of linguistic homogeneity and literary canonicity – that Barthes seeks to unseat in his critical writing. Seen from this perspective, Johnson's insistence that fissure causes fatigue aligns with these other ideas: for him, editorial insertions represent blasphemous incursions into the author's sacred ground, and interruption itself is at odds with the flowing movement of the literary utterance and the continuous development of English literature. On the other hand, Barthes's defence of disruption is a central aspect of his attack on the literary wisdom received from such figures: for Barthes, interruption helps dismantle the ideological artifice of 'literature' and engage in a more active, creative, meaningful manner with written texts.

In this chapter, I wish to extemporise on the textual phenomenon that provokes Johnson's ire – the footnote – and ask what Barthes and *Pleasure* can tell us about annotation and *vice versa*. Although it may appear perverse to consider the theme of annotation in relation to a text with only one footnote, I argue that exploring *Pleasure* in this manner can help us better understand Barthes's ideas and their relationship to his actual textual practice. According to Barthes's fellow structuralist, Gérard Genette, a footnote is an example of a 'paratext': his label for those elements of the book – such as titles, forewords, epigraphs and footnotes – that mediate between reader and text, in his influential study *Paratexts: Thresholds of Interpretation* (1987, Eng. trans. 2001). Genette insists that 'the implicit creed and spontaneous ideology of the paratext' is always 'the authorial point of view'.[5] To what extent do Barthes's paratexts confirm this claim, and to what degree do they challenge it, and adopt a more Barthesian position, complicating or undermining authorial authority? In the next section, I consider the relationship between Genette and Barthes, before examining the theme of annotation in relation to the style and claims of *Pleasure*, arguing that an unacknowledged affinity exists between Barthes's claims and the act of footnoting. I will then consider the paratextual structure of *Pleasure* and Barthes's works more widely, so as better to understand the extent to which Barthes's texts exemplify his convictions. In the last section, I ask if Barthes's tmetic aesthetic is as liberating as he believes it to be. At stake is not simply the issue of whether Barthes's texts are consistent with his critical insights, but the more important question of the value of Barthes to us today: whether his writings are refrigerated in their own time as historical documents; or whether they continue to interrupt us, to speak beyond their immediate situation, and elicit new insights.

The Solitary Footnote: The Author in the Paratext

In many ways, Barthes and Genette may be regarded as intellectual bedfellows: in a footnote to 'Introduction to the Structural Analysis of Narratives', Barthes cites approvingly Genette's distinction between 'ornamental and significant' levels of discourse, claiming that '[t]he second clearly relates to the level of story; the first to that of the discourse'.[6] Likewise, Genette uses Barthes's writing as one of his sources in *Paratexts*, using *A Lover's Discourse* as an example of his claim that 'notes are still placed in margins'. The pair share an interest in structuralism and a certain mischievous delight in bizarre metaphors and off-hand humour.

---

5   Gérard Genette, *Paratexts: Thresholds of Interpretation*, trans. by Jane E. Lewin (Cambridge: Cambridge University Press, 2001), p. 408.
6   Roland Barthes, 'Introduction to the Structural Analysis of Narratives' (1966), in *Image-Music-Text: Selected Essays*, trans. by Stephen Heath (New York: Hill and Wang, 1978), pp. 79–124 (p. 96).

Genette describes notes as 'crumbly, not to say dust-like' and jokes that 'Gérard Wajeman's novel *L'Interdit* (1986) consists solely of notes for an absent text – that was bound to happen someday'. Moreover, both express distaste for *petit bourgeois* parochialism. For instance, in an allusion to the populist mid-twentieth-century politician Pierre Poujade (who sought to defend the interests of small businessmen with a mixture of tax-cuts, nationalism and an assertion of 'common sense' over intellectualism) Genette claims that '[h]atred of notes is one of the most unchanging stereotypes of a certain anti-intellectual *Poujadisme*'.[7]

Ultimately, however, the ideas Barthes expresses about the status and nature of textuality are inconsistent with Genette's structuralism. Famously, Barthes argues that, rather than endeavour to grasp a coherent or official meaning within the text, we should abandon ourselves to its language, thereby opening ourselves to the self-transcendence made possible by the reading process: '[t]ext means Tissue; but whereas hitherto we have always taken this tissue as a product, a ready-made veil, behind which lies, more or less hidden, meaning (truth), we are now emphasizing, in the tissue, the generative idea that the text is made, is worked out in a perpetual interweaving: lost in the tissue – this texture – the subject unmakes himself, like a spider dissolving in the constructive secretions of its web' (64). Reading *Pleasure* against *Paratexts* helps us to identify one of the latter's crucial weaknesses: that Genette always envisages the paratext as a protective location, guarding an authorial meaning, never a generative one. Ostensibly, this appears to be the case: annotation, for example, asserts the empirical reality of descriptions made and lends cultural capital to the text as a whole. Yet, as I will show, the paratext enables the inclusion of collaborative or competing voices of editors, translators, creative or political partners or rivals and intertexts. Such sites do not simply extend, modulate or ramify the text, but often exceed it, introducing additional possibilities and ideas often at variance with the sentiments expressed in the centre. Instead of always reinforcing the divisions between author, reader and text, paratexts can help dissolve them, presenting the writer as a reader and analyst of their own work and thereby encouraging the reader to adopt a

7   Genette, *Paratexts*, p. 320, p. 319, p. 322, p. 319.

more active, writerly stance towards a text made up of fragments. Rather than conceiving of the paratext as a barrier, we might instead regard it in a more Barthesian fashion: as a series of waves radiating from the text, dispersing author, text and reader.

In the discontinuities they create in the text, footnotes thereby embody the aesthetic of ludic incongruity and voyeuristic disassociation Barthes avows in *Pleasure*. In the same manner as the fragmentary structure of *Pleasure* asserts the value of discontinuity, so the piecemeal, punctuating nature of footnotes disavows interpretative foreclosure, providing a 'teeming flux' (8) of languages, texts, voices and traditions; an atopic 'image-reservoir' (16) within the text; 'a powerful gush of words, a ribbon or infra-language' (7). In contrast, however, with Barthes's celebration of tmesis, many writers regard the interruption of a footnote or endnote to be an aesthetic evil, describing them for instance as 'an aberration', 'a fetish' and 'an excrescence'.[8] The English playwright and actor Noel Coward once compared reading a footnote to having to go downstairs to answer the doorbell, while making love.[9] If, as Barthes claims in *Pleasure*, when skimming the 'main' text, 'we resemble a spectator in a nightclub who climbs onto the stage and speeds up the dancer's striptease' (11), when reading footnotes we might be compared with an onlooker who departs towards the beginning of the striptease dutifully to take the stripper's clothes to a laundromat only to find that the striptease is over when they return. Yet despite their associations with drab routine, footnotes are strikingly pervasive in world literature. To take just a few examples from some of the French writers cited by Barthes in *Pleasure*, consider the footnotes in Stendhal's *The Red and the Black* (1830), Honoré de Balzac's *Father Goriot* (1835), Jules Verne's *From the Earth to the Moon* (1865), even Phillipe Sollers' *Event* (1965). In the latter

---

8   Thomas McGrath, 'Ode for the American Dead in Korea', *New and Selected Poems* (Ohio: Swallow Press, 1964), line 12; Sari Benstock, 'At the Margin of Discourse: Footnotes in the Fictional Text', *PMLA*, vol. 98, n°2 (1983), pp. 204–25 (p. 204); Thomas De Quincey, 'Style: Part One', in Thomas De Quincey, *The Collected Works of Thomas De Quincey. Volume X: Literary Theory and Criticism*, ed. by David Masson (Edinburgh: Black, 1990), p. 166.

9   Quoted in Glen W. Bowersock, 'The Art of the Footnote', *The American Scholar*, vol. 53, n°1 (1984), pp. 54–62 (p. 54).

case, Barthes even goes as far to reproduce Sollers' annotations in his approving essay 'Event, Poem, Novel' (1965). As paratexts scorned yet avidly deployed, footnotes' aberrant status hints at their Barthesian subversive potential, existing as a subterranean flow within literature, breaking at textual boundaries, threatening to overwhelm texts, readers and writers within a superabundance of commentary and intertextuality.

While Coward's above comment appears to associate footnotes with drudgery, other, more perverse, readings are possible: is not this scenario of *coitus interruptus* a common plotline in pornographic films? In such cases, rather than dissipating bliss, the entry of additional elements accentuates it ('Do you remember how exciting it was when we were making love, only to be interrupted by the doorbell'). Sometimes the original love-object is even replaced by its perverse supplement ('I was relieved from the boredom of making love again by the excitement of answering the doorbell'). To answer the doorbell while making love (note that the grammar of the original anecdote leaves unclear whether the love-making is suspended or continued during the response) is to answer the call of the despised and desired stranger. In this sense, what both footnotes and perversity share is an openness to the Other, no matter how miscellaneous, tangential or abject. The podophiliac pleasure afforded by reading and writing footnotes is linked to this textual baseness, since the abject footnote is a piece of the text, existing on its boundary, which the text has demarcated as unsuitable for full incorporation within itself; a remnant neither cherished nor abandoned, infringing upon the text by threatening to reveal the instability of its own foundations and thus the insubstantiality of its own being. Footnotes thereby encourage a perverse style of reading that exemplifies many of the critical convictions Barthes asserts in *Pleasure*.

Furthermore, in *Pleasure*, Barthes's unconventional writing style has much in common with conventional annotation. Just as annotation provides an entry-point at which the text is placed in direct conversation with other intertexts and discourses, so *Pleasure* is written from the interstices between several distinctive discourses (Christian mysticism, linguistics, literary criticism, philosophy, psychoanalysis, Zen Buddhism). Similarly, in their frequent quotation and allusion to additional intertexts, footnotes allow writers to establish a literary and intellectual context in which their work might be located. More than simply enabling a writer to accrue kudos by demonstrating their erudition, such citations invest further cultural capital in the texts they mention, situating the works to which they refer as higher authorities or worthy opponents. With its dense citationality, *Pleasure* resembles annotation and Barthes establishes a personal canon in a manner similar to that created typically within annotation. In the main, Barthes's selection is French in focus: a combination of classics (Balzac; Hugo; Flaubert; Lautréamont; Mallarmé; Maupassant; Proust; Rabelais; Stendhal; Valéry; Verne; Zola); French avant-garde writers and theorists of his time (Bachelard; Bataille; Lacan; Sollers); writers who immigrated to France (Madame de Staël; Green; Kristeva; Ségur); and artists and musicians (Cézanne; Debussy; Matisse). Other sources are primarily German (Büchner; Brecht; Heidegger; Leibniz; Marx; Murnau; Nietzsche; Silesius), secondarily British (Bacon; Dickens; Hobbes) and then either American (Poe, Chomsky) or deriving from another European nation (Cervantes; Freud; Tolstoy; van Ginneken). Aside from his various references to Zen, there are few allusions to non-Western literature, apart from fleeting nods to the Cuban writer Severo Sarduy and the *Kama Sutra*. From this we might conclude that Barthes's range of reference is surprisingly parochial, limited largely to French high culture, with token gestures to the middle-brow (Verne) practitioners working in more contemporary forms (Murnau) and the non-European. Nonetheless, Barthes's frequent references to other writers serve his broader ideas by creating an 'open' text that does not contain a single 'meaning' for them to uncover, but rather offers the opportunity to create new meanings via its multiple relationships with other texts.

Despite the accordance between Barthes's ideas and annotation and the annotative style of *Pleasure*, Barthes includes only one footnote in the volume. This apparently undistinguished appendage reads as follows:

'Episodes de la vie d'Athanase Auger, publiés par sa nièce', in *Mémoires d'un touriste*, I, pp. 238–45 (Stendhal, *Complete Works*, Calmann-Lévy, 1891). (35)

At first glance, this seems to be a fairly typical scholarly annotation, supplying such details as author (Stendhal), title (*Mémoires d'un touriste*), volume number (I), page numbers (pp. 238–45), publisher (Calmann-Levy) and year of publication (1891). By citing this quote, Barthes appears to apportion literary ownership of these words to Stendhal and thus attribute himself authorial proprietorship of the rest of the text. However, if we consider this detail more closely, it reveals itself to be more unorthodox. As Barthes acknowledges in the 'main' text, rather than cite a text written by Stendhal, the theorist refers to 'a text *cited by* Stendhal' [my italics], thereby drawing attention to the extent to which the classic nineteenth-century author's texts are themselves collections of quotations not the spontaneous outpourings of their ostensive creator's imagination. Moreover, 'Stendhal' is itself a pseudonym, and, as such, troubles the distinction between the authorial presence posited within the text and the actual historical personage with which we associate it. At the same time, the expression 'publiés par sa nièce' muddles the identity of the author of the text cited by Stendhal: does this mean the author is Auger, his niece or a different person altogether? In fact, a search on the *Bibliothèque nationale de France* catalogue reveals no entry for a text entitled 'Episodes de la vie d'Athanase Auger', suggesting that the work was Stendhal's invention. And if we consult the relevant passage in Stendhal, we find that he introduces this text in a highly convoluted manner: '[v]oici un récit textuellement copié du supplément au Constitutionnel du 19 novembre 1837' ['Here is a story literally copied from a supplement to the journal *Constitutionnel* dated 10 November 1837' (*my translation*)].[10] In a proto-Derridean deferral, Stendhal quotes not from the volume itself, nor its purported reproduction in an issue of *Constitutionnel*, but from a supplement to this French newspaper. With this annotation then, Barthes appears to pull at a loose thread within Stendhal's text, so as to unwind it. Typically, modern scholarly annotation assigns quotations to a specific author, editor or identifiable group of individuals. With this footnote, however, Barthes seems to join a teasing game of misdirection apparently initiated by Stendhal. Furthermore, in the 'main' text of *Pleasure*, Barthes claims that, in the passage cited, he hears the voice of a completely different writer altogether, exclaiming 'I find Proust' (p. 35). While Genette argues that the authorial point of view is the paratext's tacit belief, here

---

10   Stendhal [*né* Marie-Henri Beyle], *Mémoires d'un touriste* (Paris: Le Divan, 1929 [1838]), p. 380.

Barthes's note dissolves authorial ownership and thereby circumvents and challenges implicitly this latent dogma.

Barthes's hesitation over annotation continues in other works. While the essays contained in the English-language anthology of Barthes's essays *Image-Music-Text* (Eng. trans. 1977) feature a relatively hefty crop of 121 Barthes-authored footnotes, *Writing Degree Zero* (1953; Eng. trans. 1977) has a yield of only six and *Empire of Signs* (1970; Eng. trans. 1983) and *Camera Lucida: Reflections on Photography* (1980; Eng. trans. 1982) have none at all. In those relatively rare texts to which Barthes does add footnotes, he does so occasionally and with his characteristic blend of irascibility, nonchalance and mischief. In the essay accompanying *Mythologies* (1957; Eng. trans. 1972) 'Myth Today', after observing that French bourgeois society is surprisingly explicit about its own capitalist values, he adds in the margins the derisive quotation: ' "[t]he fate of capitalism is to make the worker wealthy", *Paris-Match* tells us'.[11] Barthes's omission of specific citation details render unclear as to whether he is quoting from a specific article, or simply summarising the general attitude of the popular French magazine. Such asides position the reader as a co-conspirator within his broader assault on *petit bourgeois* complacency and anti-intellectualism.

Those works in *Image-Music-Text* that Barthes annotates more prolifically tend to be more conventionally scholarly and structuralist in approach, yet his annotations nonetheless emphasise the transitional status of his writing. In 'Introduction to the Structural Analysis of Narratives' (1966; Eng. trans. 1977), Barthes adds a footnote to his distinction between 'distributional' units of narrative, events that anticipate a further occurrence in the way that 'picking up the telephone' matches a later moment at which the device is put down; and 'integrational' units that link the psychology of characters or details of context or atmosphere in the manner that a large number of telephones implies 'the power of the administrative machine behind Bond'. Barthes labels the latter '*indices*' so as to stress their role in arranging a narrative, signalling generic expectations and demarcating the

---

11   Roland Barthes, *Mythologies: The Complete Edition, in a New Translation*, trans. by Richard Howard and Annette Lavers (New York: Hill and Wang, 2013), p. 234, p. 249.

relationship between characters and their broader context. He nonetheless qualifies this classification not once but twice, adding a parenthesis in which he describes them as indices 'in the broadest sense of the word' and a further footnote, in which he states that '[t]hese designations, like those that follow, may all be provisional'.[12] Such unfolding equivocations render the text a mobile work-in-progress rather than a static summary of his ideas.

In like manner, he closes his famous essay 'Mythology Today' with a confessional footnote, in which he admits:

> Even here, in these mythologies, I have used trickery: finding it painful constantly to work on the evaporation of reality, I have started to make it excessively dense, and to discover surprising compactness in it, which I have savoured, and I have given a few examples of "substantial psychoanalysis" about some mythical objects.[13]

Here, Barthes confesses to having given weight and authority to the consumer-culture artefacts that he famously takes as his objects of analysis, and thus also potentially strengthening the ideologies they embody. Yet the impish glee with which he relishes the apparent solidity acquired by these mythologies and the ideologies they inhere undermines the substantiality he claims he apportions to them. While a more conventional radical might attempt to explode these densities, and thus aim to destroy the ideologies they contain, Barthes's more perverse approach dissolves them by approaching their very apparent concreteness as an aesthetic quality. This not only has the effect of empowering the cultural and ideological analyst, by emphasising their agency in selecting and appreciating the myths of our time. More importantly, the ludic position adopted by Barthes makes it impossible to take either them or their ideologies seriously. Far from asserting his own authorial control of the volume, here Barthes uses this footnote to undermine his own authority, revealing his own occasional deceitfulness in a manner that nonetheless suggests less embarrassment and more delight in his own ingenuity. The spirited and whimsical manner in which he expresses this encourages the reader continue the project of playfully exposing mythologies.

12 Roland Barthes, 'Introduction', *Image-Music-Text*, all quotes, p. 92.
13 Barthes, *Mythologies*, p. 274.

Barthes also displays a sophisticated understanding of the role of paratexts in creating meaning. For instance, in his essay 'The Photographic Message' (1961) he observes that 'the structure of the photograph is not an isolated structure; it is in communication with at least one structure, namely the text – title, caption or article – accompanying every press photograph.'[14] Likewise, in the epigraph to *Empire of Signs*, he informs us that:

> The text does not 'gloss' the images, which do not 'illustrate' the text. For me, each has been no more than the onset of a kind of visual uncertainty, analogous perhaps to that *loss of meaning* Zen calls a *satori*. Text and image, interlacing, seek to ensure the circulation and exchange of these signifiers: body, face, writing; and in them to read the retreat of signs.[15]

Here Barthes resists according ancillary, paratextual status to either text or image, instead entwining them in an ambiguous relationship that facilitates different forms of interchange between the signs contained within them. Rather than seal the text within a singular monological intention, the gloss adds an additional textual surface that compounds the work's heteroglossic complexity.

In keeping with this, his texts frequently have unusual and complex textual structures. As a series of ninety-seven textual fragments, separated into groups of one to five by a line of three titles, *Pleasure* resembles more closely hypertext than a conventional 'main' text with paratextual additions. Intriguingly, Barthes provides section-headings in the 'Contents' page, but not within the sections themselves. This compounds the sense of slippage between sections, as if they are not discrete territories demarcated by their corresponding label, but intersecting areas, with multiple porous connections to one another. The effort of flipping back and forth between 'Contents' and text also discourages the reader from relating each section to its title, effectively playing down the sense that there exists a central plan 'within' the work and encouraging an active, independent reading. Barthes also adds an epigraph that exists in a decidedly ambiguous

14   Roland Barthes, 'The Photographic Message' (1961), in *Image-Music-Text*, pp. 15–31 (p. 16).
15   Barthes, *Empire of Signs*, p. xi.

relationship with the rest of the text. In the French original, this appears as '[l]a seule passion de ma vie a été la peur' ['[m]y one passion in life has been fear'].[16] And the English translation provides the same quotation in the original latin:

> Atque metum tatum concepit tunc mea mater
>
> *Ut paraete geminos, meque metumque simul.*
>
> ['My mother bore me and fear as twins together' (my translation)]

> – Hobbes (xi)

In the text itself, Barthes refers to these lines seemingly only in passing: when contemplating the '[p]roximity […] of bliss and fear', he proposes that 'fear is the misfit of every philosophy (except, I believe, Hobbes' remark that the one passion of his life had been fear)' (48). According to Barthes, 'anxiety' can be considered a 'noble word' (48) perhaps due to the role it plays in the philosophy of Søren Kierkegaard, Freudian psychoanalysis and existentialism, but fear lacks this metaphysical provenance. Despite this, Barthes claims, fear and *jouissance* parallel one another in being furtive, intensely personal, almost transcendent experiences that have the effect of 'splitting the subject *while leaving him intact*' (48). Fear is therefore a misfit not simply in being ignored, but also in the more important sense of being antipathetical towards the Cartesian thrust of modern philosophical thought. In this passage, Barthes's use of Hobbes' lines portrays fear not only as a guiding force of the life of a philosopher with direct experience of the English Civil War (and even the death threats that greeted the publication of *Leviathan* (1651)) but as an alternative source of inspiration for philosophy, a consideration underscored by his inclusion of the quotation as epigraph. Yet fear is by no means an overt themes of *Pleasure*, and the reader is left to wonder why Barthes chooses to quote an English philosopher best known for both his support for royal absolutism and his development of some of the fundamentals of European liberal thought. Such obscurity (accentuated in the English translation by

16   Roland Barthes, *Le Plaisir du texte* (Paris: Seuil, 1973), p. 7.

the quotation being presented in the original Latin) serves the Barthesian purpose of compelling the reader to look outside the text to intertexts when making interpretative choices. For Barthes, the act of riffling through the paratexts and parentheses, establishing new connections and demarcating fresh meanings is more important than the actual connections or meanings delineated: the process is crucial, not the end result – and his paratexts for *Pleasure* manifest this.

Pleasure is not the only essay in which Barthes creates an unconventional textual structure to encourage active, intertextual reading. Although the subtitle of *A Lover's Discourse* (1977) is *Fragments*, Barthes structures the text in a highly organised albeit unconventional manner. He links titles to explanatory headnotes that sometimes define, sometimes extend and comment upon the title to which they are appended. He numbers small sections of one or two paragraphs and attaches to them on the side of the page by an elliptical marginal gloss in which he displays abbreviated names of authors and titles of books. In a further, still more unusual marginal gloss, he provides the names of authors and sometimes the names of the works to which he refers, at others a quotation. These glosses lack the specificity of conventional scholarly annotation (no name of translator, editor or publisher, place or year of publication or page number), instead encouraging the reader to bring to mind their memory of reading the text in question, rather than consulting it directly, and to linger on the text's surfaces. In one note, for example, Barthes half-cites Fyodor Dostoyevsky's *The Brothers Karamazov* (1880) before reminiscing: '[t]he death of Father Zossima: the noxious smell of the corpse'.[17]

Such discursive, often eccentric glosses recall the playful italicised quotations and comments Barthes adds to the photographs in his famous *Camera Lucida* (1980). Alongside an 1857 portrait of the French author and poet Marceline Desbordes-Valmore taken by the French photographer 'Nadar' [*né* Gaspard-Félix Tournachon], Barthes not only inscribes the minimalist citation 'NADAR: MARCELINE DESBORDES-VALMORE. 1857' but adds the supercilious comment '*Marceline Desbordes-Valmore*

---

17   Roland Barthes, *A Lover's Discourse: Fragments*, trans. by Richard Howard (London: Vintage, 1978), p. 25.

reproduces in her face the slightly stupid virtues of her verses …'.[18] By teasingly deflating the melancholy dignity to which Desbordes-Valmore aspires, Barthes here articulates what he describes in his essay 'The Third Meaning' as 'the obtuse meaning' of the image.[19] The interstitial position of the paratextual caption provides Barthes with the opportunity to elicit these esoteric, eccentric meanings, dangling readers between the inside and outside of the text, the image and its inscription into writing, and thereby encouraging us to register more fully the sensuous, physical details of the images and texts under consideration.

Perhaps most provocatively, in *S/Z: An Essay* (1970), Barthes inverts the conventional relationship between text and paratext: in the English translation, Barthes's commentary thrusts itself centre-stage; while the ostensive object of his analysis, Honoré de Balzac's short story *Sarrasine* (1830) retreats to the back-stage location of an Appendix. By treating Balzac's text in this manner, Barthes rescues a traditional realist work from being a reductive 'readerly' text closed to multiple interpretations, and refashions it into a 'writerly' one, open to an infinity of intertextual exchanges. Barthes describes the latter in the following manner:

> this text is a galaxy of signifiers, not a structure of signifieds; it has no beginning; it is reversible; we gain access to it by several entrances, none of which can be authoritatively declared to be the main one; the code it mobilizes extend *as far as the eye can reach* … there is never *a whole* of the text.

Barthes's distinction between 'readerly' and 'writerly' texts is often understood to relate to the difference between, on the one hand, the univocality of nineteenth-century realism and most commercial literature and, on the other, the polyvocality of the twentieth-century *avant-garde*. However, by using his own commentary to deconstruct and reconstruct Balzac's supposedly 'readerly' text, Barthes complicates this distinction, demonstrating that the act of annotation provides a means of opening new

18 Roland Barthes, *Camera Lucida: Reflections on Photography* (London: Vintage, 1981), p. 101.
19 Roland Barthes, 'The Third Meaning: Research Notes on Some Eisenstein Stills' (1970), in *Image-Music-Text*, pp. 52–68 (p. 61).

creative and interpretative possibilities. Indeed, Barthes himself observes this consideration, reminding us that, in contrast to the flexibility and mobility of the writerly text, 'the classic text is incompletely reversible (it is modestly plural)' but asserting that 'the step-by-step commentary is of necessity a renewal of entrances to the text, it avoids structuring the text excessively, avoids giving it that additional structure which would come from a dissertation and would close it: it stars the text, instead of assembling it.'[20] Here Barthes is attempting to account for his decision to present his analysis in the form of a combination of short, discursive essays and 561 annotations marking and interrupting Balzac's original work. But his disclosures also offer us insights into how annotation helps open a text to interpretation and intertextual play, rather than organising it into a singular, narrow explanation.

For Barthes, such disruptions allow us to adopt an active, analytical standpoint in relation to the text and the ideologies it puts forward, in contrast to the passivity encouraged by conventional realist representation. In a memorably bizarre, almost mystical passage, Barthes announces that 'like the soothsayer drawing on it [i.e. the sky] with the tip of his staff an imaginary rectangle wherein to consult, according to certain principles, the flight of birds, the commentator traces through the text certain zones of reading, in order to observe therein the migration of meanings, the outcropping of codes, the passage of citations'.[21] Barthes's ethnographic imagery and effusive dizeugma accord an almost mystical significance to the act of commentary. To annotate with analysis is to render the apparently static meaning of a text mobile and place it in relation to a multiplicity of languages and intertexts. As Barthes himself acknowledges, the commentary therefore necessarily adopts a partly antagonistic, even destructive, attitude towards the text. He observes that 'the work of commentary, once it is separated from any ideology of totality, consists precisely in *manhandling* the text, *interrupting* it'.[22] By affirming the existence of plural interpretations,

---

20   Roland Barthes, *S/Z: An Essay* (1970), trans. by Richard Miller (New York: Hill and Wang, 1974), pp. 5–6 (p. 13).

21   Barthes, *S/Z*, p. 14.

22   *Ibid.*, pp. 14–5.

rejecting ideas of totality and completion and disrupting the syntactical and rhetorical flow of the text, annotation opens the text to the reader.

In contrast to Barthes's own attempts to use his paratexts to open his work, other paratexts contained within his printed works seek often to close his writing, subordinating it to a concept of a legitimate authorial interpretation. On the front page of *Pleasure*, for example, the authorial signature 'Roland Barthes' stands above the title, in letters of the same length, while the name of the translator appears in considerably smaller writing at the bottom. On the inside page, the list of '*Books by Roland Barthes*' places *Pleasure* within an authorial canon. In 'A Note on the Text', Richard Howard reassures us that, although the text may appear discontinuous and disconnected, in fact it follows a clear authorial design immanent within the work that can be recognised and articulated by readers: '[l]ike filings which gather to form a figure in a magnetic field, the parts and pieces here do come together' (vii). On the back page, a summary of Barthes's biography (when he was born, where he studied, taught and researched, when he died) attaches the text to the life of its producer. The accompanying black-and-white photograph of Barthes peering enigmatically towards us in front of a bookshelf with the right-hand side of his face in shadow (hinting at mystery and mischief) provides visual reassurance that the text comprises the utterance of an identifiable historical personage.

Even the extract from Susan Sontag's essay 'Writing Itself' (1982) that provides *Pleasure*'s blurb presents the text as an example of a distinctive authorial commitment to playfulness:

> Barthes repeatedly compared teaching to play, reading to eros, writing to seduction [...]. All of Barthes' work is an exploration of the histrionic or ludic.

This excerpt also locates the text within a narrative of Barthes's intellectual development as a writer: '[h]is voice became more and more personal'.[23] While Sontag's and Howard's comments are clearly intended to communicate Barthes's merits to an Anglophone audience, the effect is to constrict the text within an authorial meaning. In a contradiction that may

---

23   Susan Sontag, 'Writing Itself: On Roland Barthes', in *A Barthes Reader*, ed. by Susan Sontag (New York: Hill and Wang, 1982), p. xvi.

have amused or alarmed Barthes himself a team of editors, translators, critics and interpreters are required to forge and promote 'Barthes the author'.

Must We Burn Barthes? The Politics of Interruption

An examination of Barthes's paratexts reveal a central tension existing within English-language editions of his work: while editors have be-atified Barthes as a canonical author, Barthes's own critical claims and paratextual practices resist such anointment. Indeed, it is possible that his scant use of annotation results from a perhaps unconscious suspicion about a practice that is so frequently used to consecrate a writer. Instead, like the famous anamorphic skull in Holbein the younger's *The Ambassadors* (1533), Barthes's droll captions, rebarbative footnotes and whimsical glosses frame his work from a side-view, compelling the reader to regard the text from an unfamiliar angle, and complicating any attempt to assign a singular meaning to the text by reshaping it into a dialogue between two or more competing structures. While Genette insists that the paratext always facilitates a more coherent, authorial reading of the text, Barthes's paratexts instead perform the action of 'splitting the subject, while leaving him intact' (48).

Nonetheless, annotation challenges several of Barthes's claims, in particular his distinction between a first-order denotative style of reading and a second-order connotative approach. Barthes describes 'two systems of reading; one goes straight to the articulation of the anecdote, it considers the extent of the text, ignores the play of language … the other reading skips nothing; it weighs, it sticks to the text, it reads, so to spark, with application and transport, grasps at every point in the text the asyndeton which cuts the various languages' (12). Annotation, however, allows both of these forms of reading to exist simultaneously: the 'main' text can offer extensive purposive reading, the notes a more intensive, analytical approach to the same text. In this sense, annotation provides a further layer of cognitive dissonance overlooked by Barthes in *Pleasure*, nonetheless exemplifying and extending his aesthetic of interruption.

A closer consideration of the development of annotation also demonstrates to the limitations of Barthes's historical purview. For example, in *Pleasure*, Barthes claims that the writing of Gustave Flaubert's obsessive interest in style marked a major departure in literary realism, and in literature more widely: 'with Flaubert, for the first time, discontinuity is no longer exceptional, sporadic, brilliant' (9). Barthes's belief that a shift in nineteenth-century French literature marks a world aesthetic revolution betrays his own parochialism (what about other European literature, never mind the literatures of other continents?). But if we include the margins of literary texts within our understanding of French literature of this period, we can also see that discontinuity and the practice of engaging in complex transactions in the interstitial spaces within the text is common within, if not intrinsic to, the writing of the major French realists. For example, we might consider a footnote in Stendhal's *The Red and the Black* (1830) in which the writer compares the hero Julien Sorel's expression with the Italian baroque paintings of Giovanni Francesco Barbieri: '[s]ee in the Louvre museum, François, Duke of Aquitaine, laying down his breastplate and donning a monk's habit'.[24] The note ostensibly seeks to bolster the novel's claims to provide a mimetic image of French society and reality itself by providing evidence supporting the narrator's analogy. But the effect is instead to undermine verisimilitude by breaking the reader's suspension of disbelief, drawing them back to the world outside the text and thereby drawing attention to the novel's fictive, constructed status. Paying closer attention to such annotation shows us that, literary realism not only can be rewritten via annotation, but that *contra* Barthes, a steady underground stream of discontinuity coursed through it.

At the same time, considering more closely the discordant ethos espoused by Barthes and encapsulated in the footnote may make us more sceptical about the political thrust of Barthes's argument. In Barthes's view, complete, uninterrupted utterances are a bourgeois affectation that enables authority figures to present an arbitrary social system as an impermeable, unalterable reality:

24 Stendhal, *The Red and the Black*, trans. by Catherine Slater (Oxford: Oxford University Press, 1991), p. 191.

The professor is someone who finishes his sentences. The politician being interviewed clearly takes a great deal of trouble to imagine an ending to his sentence: and if he stopped short? His entire policy would be jeopardized! (51)

Breaking the text and subjecting it to analysis is therefore a radical act, because it disrupts the conventional perceptions within capitalist society. Barthes writes in 'Structural Analysis of Narratives' that '[t]he reluctance to declare its codes characterizes bourgeois society and the mass culture issuing from it; both demand signs which do not look like signs'.[25] Barthes's main target is what he describes in the 'Preface to the 1970 edition' of *Mythologies* as 'the mystification which transforms *petit bourgeois* culture into a universal nature':[26] anti-intellectualism; parochialism; *Poujadisme*. And in *Pleasure* itself, Barthes appears to call for an erotics of reading separate from the more overtly political readings that characterised earlier works, exclaiming defiantly his belief in 'our bliss [*jouissance*] in the text against the prudery of ideological analysis' (vii).

From the vantage point of the early twenty-first century, one might take issue with Barthes's choice of nemesis. *Poujadisme* may in some ways continue as a trend within French politics via Poujade's early follower and ally Jean-Marie Le Pen and his daughter and President of the French *National Front* Marine Le Pen. Nevertheless, Poujade's insular conservatism should not be conflated with the views of the contemporary French far-right. We might remark that he who goes to War with idiots risks becoming an idiot himself. Moreover, given the relatively narrow cultural range of his citations in *Pleasure*, it appears a little hypocritical for him to accuse others of insularity. Furthermore, while parochialism obviously persists, it is difficult to consider it as central a force within world politics as globalisation, the deindustrialisation of developed economies or the digitisation of everyday life. And what these contemporary fundamental phenomena have in common is a disruption and discontinuity. As the urban theorists Teresa Ebert and Mas'ud Zavarzadeh assert:

25   Barthes, 'Introduction', in *Image-Music-Text*, p. 116.
26   Barthes, 'Preface to the 1970 edition', in *Mythologies*, pp. ix–x (p. ix).

Discontinuity is valorized [...] because it maps the social as an assemblage of fragmentary and unconnected events and, among other things, represents capitalism as continuously starting a 'new' phase that enables it to disconnect itself from its exploitations in the past and always remain a 'new' capitalism.[27]

For people living in twenty-first-century advanced capitalist countries, new technologies and working practices are creating lifestyles in which interruption is not an edifying release, but a norm. Moreover, in an economic environment in which intellectual property is under increasing pressure, and collaborative forms such as films, social media and videogames provide the main forums in which people gain aesthetic experience, authorship itself looks more and more out of date. From this vantage point, then, Barthes's views appear less a subversion of capitalism's ideological superstructure, more a plan for its reinvention.

But we could even go further than this, and suggest that both Barthes's polemic and the disruptive reading style encouraged by footnotes manifest a sense of discontinuity fundamental to the experience of capitalist modernity itself. As Georg Simmel observed in his classic study of the impact of technology on the human senses, 'The Metropole and Mental Life' (1903), psychological adaptation to disruption has been a central part of urban life since the emergence of capitalism. According to him, '[t]he psychological foundation, upon which the [modern] metropolitan individuality is erected, is the intensification of emotional life due to the swift and continuous shift of external and internal stimuli'.[28] Tellingly, the early nineteenth-century British writer, Thomas De Quincey described 'the practice of footnotes' as 'a practice purely modern',[29] suggesting not only that annotation was increasingly in vogue in British letters at this time, but also that this convention (which emerged only in the eighteenth century) embodied a very modern sense of contradiction, disintegration and disunity. In this sense, both the footnote and Barthes's argument manifest

27   Teresa Ebert and Mas'ud Zavarzadeh, *Class in Culture* (Boulder: Paradigm, 2008), p. 65.
28   Georg Simmel, 'The Metropolis and Mental Life' (1903), in Gary Bridge and Sophie Watson (eds), *The Blackwell City Reader* (Oxford and Malden, MA: Wiley-Blackwell, 2002), pp. 103–10 (p. 103).
29   De Quincey, 'Style', p. 166.

and valorise a cognitive dissonance essential to capitalism's continual development: rather than critique modern capitalist society Barthes could be said to unwittingly celebrate it.

What, however, I think, prevents Barthes's fragmentary ethos from being collapsed into capitalist ideology is that he imagines a form of transformation far more profound. Capitalism may aver a rhetoric of constant revolution so as to legitimise its destructive consequences, but it is fundamentally stationary because it leaves the division between capital and labour intact: the Marseille factory may be relocated to Manilla and the power loom replaced with the Apple Mac, but the power relationship between investors and workers remains frigidly unequal. On the contrary, Barthes envisages a far more profound alteration: an interruption that dissipates fundamentally the conditions that cause it to come into being. In a quotation already cited in this essay, he asserts that 'the text is made, is worked out in a perpetual interweaving: lost in the tissue – this texture – the subject unmakes himself, like a spider dissolving in the constructive secretions of its web' (64). There are spiritual and erotic as well as literary dimensions to this image of self-abandonment. But, if we place it in a political context, Barthes's account represents a call for constant, vigilant scrutiny of the ideological foundations of our own assumptions based on an openness to the abject and alterior. What is perhaps most intriguing about it is that he envisages this revolutionary disruption as an evacuation of energy akin to a process of regelation, in which the subject is fundamentally divested of identity, rather than acquiring a new one. In this sense, *jouissance* goes hand in hand with ideological analysis rather than being opposed to it. Barthes's work thereby not only provides a series of valuable insights into Western literature and twentieth-century culture of considerable influence and importance, but also furnishes us with hints towards an idiosyncratic but compelling advocacy of revolutionary personal and political change as refrigeration via interruption.

PATRICK FFRENCH

2 *To Enter Madly into the Image*
Reading Projectively in Barthes

For Roland Barthes, reading – the reading he desires – is mobile, and erotic. Those texts that desire rather than demand to be read are texts that allow the reader to move around in them and in relation to them, that establish a space of seduction. At more extreme moments, however, and this is what I want to explore in what follows, Barthes expresses a desire for a different mode of relation to the text, a 'mad' desire to enter into the world of the text and to act in that world. I propose to call this 'projective' reading; the reader is projected into or projects him/herself into the space of the text, driven by a hallucinatory belief in the existence of this world and the beings that populate it. This begins to outline an account of reading oriented around what Barthes will call 'moments de vérité' [moments of truth] which may contrast with what we may assume to be his theory of reading as a form of structural analysis.[1] This desire to 'enter, madly' into a form is expressed in two passages that I am going to look at in detail. Perversely, they concern not literature but film, and to some extent this essay is also the basis for a project on Barthes and cinema.[2] They are,

1   See Roland Barthes, *La Préparation du roman I et II: Cours et séminaires au Collège de France (1978–1979 et 1979–1980)* (Paris: Seuil/Imec, 2003), pp. 151–61.

2   Barthes has had a profound influence on film theory, and a number of important articles have considered this topic. See, for example, Dana Polan, 'Roland Barthes and the Moving Image', *October*, vol. 18 (1981), pp. 41–6; James S. Williams, 'At the Reader's Discretion: on Barthes and Cinema', *Paragraph*, vol. 21, n°1 (1998), pp. 45–56; Victor Burgin, 'Barthes' Discretion', in Jean-Michel Rabaté (ed.), *Writing the Image After Roland Barthes* (Philadelphia: University of Pennsylvania Press, 1997), pp. 19–31; Steven Ungar, 'Persistence of the Image: Barthes, Photography and the Resistance to Film', in Diana Knight (ed.), *Critical Essays on Roland Barthes* (New York: Hamm and Co., 2000), pp. 236–49. Raymond Bellour's *L'Entre-Images*

firstly, a very short report on the then new technology of cinemascope, the essay 'Au cinémascope', published in Maurice Nadeau's review *Les Lettres nouvelles* in February 1954. The second piece is the penultimate chapter of *La Chambre claire*, in which Barthes recalls a visit to the cinema and his reaction to a sequence of Fellini's *Casanova*. These two moments, at either end, roughly, of Barthes' trajectory, establish the parameters for a possible understanding of Barthes' relation to cinema, and trace the movement between a will to enter actively into History and the will to 'enter, madly' into the spectacle and thus to intervene in the struggle against human mortality.

Onto the Stage of History

'Au Cinémascope' is the third piece Barthes devoted entirely or partially to cinema. It precedes the regular contributions to *Les Lettres nouvelles* that will appear under the heading 'Petite mythologie du mois' and which will

---

(Paris: La Différence, 2002) and *L'Entre-images* 2 (Paris: P.O.L, 2002) are imbued with the thought of Barthes. The first volume only is available in translation (by Allyn Hardyck as *Between-the-Images* (Paris: Les Presses du réel/JRP, 2012)). Bellour, Laura Mulvey and Victor Burgin have also pursued the implications of Barthes' 'resistance' to cinema because of its lack of 'pensivité'; see Raymond Bellour, 'The Pensive Spectator', in *Between-the-Images*; Laura Mulvey, 'The Possessive Spectator', and Victor Burgin, 'Possessive, Pensive and Possessed', both in David Green and Joanna Lowry (eds), *Stillness and Time: Photography and the Moving Image* (Brighton: Photoforum and Photoworks, 2006). See also Jonathan Rosenbaum's 'Barthes & Film: 12 Suggestions' (<http://www.jonathanrosenbaum.net/2018/05/barthes-film-12-suggestions-tk/>). Surprisingly, however, the relation between Barthes and cinema has not provoked a full-length study until Philipp Watt's post-humous 2015 book *Roland Barthes et le cinéma* (Paris: de l'Incidence, 2015) and conferences at the École Normale Supérieure and at the Centre Pompidou in October 2015, with an accompanying film programme (of 27 films) at the cinema Le Champo (5ème arrondissement), curated by Antoine de Baecque, Marie Gil and Éric Marty (<https://www.fabula.org/actualites/barthes-en-sortant-du-cinema_70106.php>).

be collected in the 1957 book *Mythologies*. It concerns the newly patented process for anamorphic widescreen projection originally invented as Barthes notes by a Frenchman, Henri Chrétien in 1926, but only adopted and marketed in 1953 by 20th Century Fox in the US.[3] Barthes admits that, lacking expertise, he cannot define Chrétien's invention but that he can judge its effects, thus attending to the experience of cinemascope in a quasi-phenomenological manner, as a 'user' or 'amateur' of the practice of cinema-going.[4] There is a deliberately non-scientific emphasis here – Barthes draws on an affective knowledge and experience rather than on expertise. He is concerned with the changes in spectatorship resulting from the expansion or extension of the screen, and significantly underlines the shift to the dimensions of binocular vision and the effect this has on the interior, subjective dimension of reception, arguing that cinemascope will 'fatally' transform the affectivity of cinema spectatorship: 'L'élargissement de l'image aux dimensions de la vision binoculaire doit fatalement transformer la sensibilité interne de l'amateur de cinéma' [The broadening of the image to the dimensions of binocular vision should fatally transform the internal sensibility of the filmgoer].[5] Cinema space moves towards that of theatre, but, importantly, not to the 'box' theatre 'à l'italienne' of post-nineteenth-century bourgeois theatre but to the open space of 'antique' or – as we will see 'epic', and ultimately Brechtian theatre: 'La frontalité, étendue, touche au cercle, c'est-à-dire à l'espace idéal des grandes

---

3   For an informative account of widescreen, which also considers André Bazin's response to it, see Douglas Smith, 'Reading *The Robe*: Bazin and Widescreen', in *Paragraph*, vol. 36, n°1 (2013), pp. 86–100. The new technology was welcomed (albeit for a variety of different reasons) by the *Cahiers* critics Truffaut, Rohmer and Rivette. Their writing on it is usefully collected in *Théories du cinéma: Petite anthologie des Cahiers du cinéma VII* (Paris: Cahiers du cinéma, 2001).

4   'Si je ne peux, faute de science, définir le procédé Henri Chrétien, du moins puis-je en juger les effets' [If, for lack of the proper technical background, I can't define Henri Chrétien's [anamorphic] process, at least I can judge its effects] (Roland Barthes, 'Au cinémascope', *Lettres nouvelles*, n°12 (February 1954); available in *Œuvres complètes*, Tome I, 1942–1961 (Paris: Seuil, 2002), pp. 456–7 (p. 456); translated by Jonathan Rosenbaum in *Jouvert*, vol. 3, n°3 (Spring 1999), <http://english.chass.ncsu.edu/jouvert/v3i3/barth.htm>).

5   *Ibid.*

dramaturgies' [The stretched-out frontality becomes almost circular; in other words, the ideal space of the great dramaturgies].[6] The extension or width of the screen, its frontality or surface, tends towards a curvature, a screen that surrounds rather than enclosing. This new spatial disposition, a change in what would later be called the apparatus, introduces, in Barthes' account, a crucial shift in spectatorship: 'Jusqu'ici, le regard du spectateur était celui d'un gisant souterrain, muré dans l'ombre et recevant la nourriture cinématographique à peu près comme un allongé est nourri passivement à la sonde ou à la pipette' [Up until now, the look of the spectator has been that of someone lying prone and buried, walled up in the darkness, receiving cinematic nourishment rather like the way a patient is fed intravenously or drip fed].[7] Here Barthes develops a critical and incisively ironic approach to cinematic spectatorship with the image of being fed or 'drip fed' passively. The later notion of ideological 'capture' by the screen, developed in Barthes' 1975 article 'En Sortant du cinéma' [On Leaving the Cinema] but also in articles of the early 1970s by Jean-Louis Baudry and in the journal *Cahiers du cinéma*, is evident here, already, but there is also an echo of earlier film-theoretical notions of cinema's 'hypnotic' effects.[8] With cinemascope, by contrast, the spectator is 'à un immense balcon' [on the balcony], s/he can move – 'je bouge à l'aise' [I move effortlessly], and this instigates not only a change in position but also a change of subjectivity: 'je commence à être environné et à

---

6   *Ibid.*

7   *Ibid.*

8   See Roland Barthes, 'En Sortant du cinéma', in *Le Bruissement de la langue* (Paris: Seuil, 1984), pp. 383–6. This essay was originally published in the hugely influential 1975 issue of the journal *Communications* (issue 23) convened by Raymond Bellour, Christian Metz and Thierry Kuntzel on 'Psychanalyse et cinéma'. It appears alongside Baudry's 'Le Dispositif', a development of his earlier work on the apparatus in the journal *Cinéthique*, and further important work by Metz ('Le film de fiction et son spectateur'), Kuntzel ('Le Travail du film'), Bellour, and Julia Kristeva. The materialist orientation of the review *Tel Quel* proved influential for the critics of *Cahiers du cinéma*, which in the 1970s especially entered a period of politically oriented theoretical formalism. For earlier theorisations of cinema and hypnosis, see Gilles Deleuze, *Cinéma II: L'Image-temps* (Paris: Minuit, 1985), chapter 7; Sarah Cooper, *The Soul of Film Theory* (London: Palgrave Macmillan, 2013).

substituer à ma sensibilité larvaire, l'euphorie d'une circulation égale entre le spectacle et mon corps' [I begin to be surrounded, and my larval state is replaced by the euphoria of an equal circulation between the spectacle and my body].[9] The clear opposition here is between the dependency of a 'larval' sensibility and the euphoria of a free circulation, in other words between a situation of passive dependency which is connoted as imma-ture, undeveloped, fœtal and the utopic mobility of a 'free circulation' between subject and object, an economy free of demand and subjection in which Barthes recognises happiness and which, I would suggest, cor-responds to the space of seduction and of desire he will later theorise in *Le Plaisir du texte*.[10]

Darkness itself is transformed. In the ordinary cinema darkness is a tomb; there is a strong, Poe-esque connotation of death and imprisonment, which Barthes connects to the 'mythic' space of the cave. The cave, of course, will be, in Baudry's apparatus texts, a crucial instance of cinematic illusion and obfuscation via the scene of Plato's cave.[11] Here it appears as a motif of regressive mysticism: the cinema – pre-scope – is a sacred space, thus a space of regression and mystification. In cinemascopic space, the image is not received as a series of 'lines' but as a *volume*: 'je ne reçois pas l'image par ces longs fils de lumière, que l'on voit transpercer et nourrir les stigmatisés' [I don't receive the image by those long threads of light that one sees trans-fixing and feeding the stigmatised].[12] Barthes posits the spectator of the 'ordinary' cinema as analogous to the figures in religious paintings which show rays of light piercing the virgin or the saint; the 'stigmatised' subject is both nourished and wounded by the image (contrasting interestingly with the later poetics of the *punctum* in *La Chambre claire*), again under-lining the sense of regressive dependency. In scopic space, however, I am able to stretch out along the length of the screen: 'je m'accoude à même la longueur du spectacle', translated as 'I lean forward on my elbows, be-coming as horizontal as the spectacle'.[13] Barthes posits with cinemascope a

9   Barthes, 'Au cinémascope', p. 456.
10 See Roland Barthes, *Le Plaisir du texte* (Paris: Seuil, 1973), pp. 13–4.
11 See Jean-Louis Baudry, 'Le Dispositif', *Communications*, n°23 (1975), pp. 56–72.
12 Barthes, 'Au cinémascope', p. 456.
13 *Ibid.*

capacity for the spectator to spread themselves out, and instead of a larvae, become a God, via the new dimensions of equality with the image: I am no longer 'under' the image, but in front of it, amidst it; I am no longer separated from it by the distance of a look, but in some sense engaged in it through the 'ideal distance' of creation – the reach of the arm.[14] Here Barthes incorporates a Merleau-Pontyesque motif of chiasmatic immersion in the world through gesture and reach, breaking down the distance and abstraction of sight alone. This wider space, Barthes proposes, will have to be occupied differently; the close-up may not survive; kisses, sweating, psychology, all of this will recede into the shadows.[15] The new space will instigate a new dialectic between man and objects, a dialectic of solidarity. The spectator will be elbow to elbow with the revolutionary workers of *Battleship Potemkin*, writes Barthes, and Man will finally step on the stage of History and enter the epic dimension of action.[16]

Who is speaking here? Is this unashamedly Marxist, utopian vision of an egalitarian, participatory spectatorship intended entirely without the usual irony that accompanies Barthes' mythologies, the second voice that

14   '[…] de larve, je deviens un peu dieu puisque me voici, non plus sous l'image, mais devant elle, au milieu d'elle, séparé d'elle par cette distance idéale du bras (Dieu et les peintres ont toujours le bras long)' [out of my larval state emerge as a little god because here I am, no longer under the image but in front of it, in the middle of it, separated from it by this ideal distance, necessary to creation, which is no longer that of the glance but that of the arm's reach (God and painters always have outstretched arms)] (*ibid.*).

15   'L'espace plus large, il faudra évidemment l'occuper de nouvelle manière; il se peut que le gros plan ne survive pas, tout au moins modifie sa fonction: baisers, sueurs, psychologie, tout cela réintégrera peut-être l'ombre et le lointain' [Obviously one must occupy the largest space in a new manner; perhaps the close-up will not survive, or at least its function will be transformed: kisses, sweat, psychology may all reinstate darkness and distance] (*ibid.*).

16   '[…] une nouvelle dialectique entre les hommes et l'horizon, entre les hommes et les objets, doit surgir, une dialectique de la solidarité et non plus du décor. Ceci devrait être, à proprement parler, l'espace de l'Histoire et, techniquement, la dimension épique est née' [a new dialectic between men and the horizon, men and objects, should come into view, a dialectic of interdependence and no longer one of décor. Properly speaking, this should be the space of History, and technically, the epic dimension is born] (*ibid.*).

one can hear alongside the first? I would suggest that Barthes does fully intend this utopian vision, but the irony, the demystificatory instance lies in the distance between the kind of spectatorship that the technology might make possible, according to Barthes, and the reality of its contemporary usage. It is an irony that expresses a wish. Barthes ends the article by wondering what will be shown via Scope – 'Reste à savoir ce qu'on nous y montrera : si ce sera *Potemkine* ou *La Tunique*, Odessa ou Saint-Sulpice, l'Histoire ou la Mythologie' [What remains to be seen is what we'll be shown there; if it will be Potemkin or *The Robe*, Odessa or Saint-Sulpice, History or Mythology].[17] In fact Henry Koster's film *The Robe*, starring Richard Burton, Jean Simmons and Victor Mature, was marketed by 20th Century Fox as 'the first Motion Picture in Cinemascope', and was distributed and shown in Europe under the title *La Tunique*. What Barthes wonders – what he says remains to be seen is already the case, as he well knows. What he marks here, then, is something like a missed opportunity to enter into the image and into history, a distance between a utopic vision and the alienated and mystified reality of the contemporary moment.

So is the question Barthes asks at the end of 'Au cinémascope' – Eisenstein or Hollywood – real or rhetorical? Does he believe in the possibility of a participatory, active spectatorship, of entering onto 'the stage of History', or is this (merely) a utopian fantasy, the abandoned hope of an already melancholic Marxism? Barthes' enthusiasm for the Théâtre National Populaire, and the 'bedazzlement' (*éblouissement*) he reported on first seeing Brecht's Berliner Ensemble perform in Paris, suggests that at this stage Barthes believes that the possibilities of critical action 'in' History have not yet been exhausted.[18] However, this hope is short-lived, I would suggest. The notion of a participatory, historically active spectatorship will be absent from Barthes' writing in the 1960s, from the structuralist and semiological phases of his trajectory, however much these move against the doxa. The image is situated in this period in the domain of the Imaginary,

17   *Ibid.*
18   See Roland Barthes, 'Éblouissement', in *Le Bruissement de la langue*, pp. 199–200. For Barthes' involvement in the group TNP and writing on theatre in the 1950s, see Diana Knight, *Barthes and Utopia: Space, Travel, Writing* (Oxford: Clarendon, 1997), chapter 1, 'Making Space'.

of misrecognition and ideological unification, as against the plural and material realm of the Text as explored in books such as *S/Z*. There is fruitful terrain to explore in the ways that Barthes' approach to the text as an active 'structuration' (a process of structuring rather than a fixed structure) influences film analysis, particularly in the work of Metz, Bellour and Kuntzel. Here the de-structuring of the film in the process of analysis points to what Kuntzel calls the 'film-work', the transformative process that works between the film in the can and the film as projected.[19] This is also a mode of 'entering in' to the image, and this kind of work is visible in Barthes' essay of the early 1970s, 'Le Troisième sens' [The Third meaning].[20] But one must wait, I would suggest, until *La Chambre claire* to see a fuller articulation of Barthes 'projective' relation to the image.

Champ aveugle / Hors-champ

La Chambre claire was the second publication in the book series that Jean Narboni launched in the early 1980s for *Cahiers du cinéma*.[21] Narboni approached Barthes with the idea of writing a book for the Cahiers series, a commission to which Barthes responded, after some delays, with the book to which he gave the subtitle 'Note sur la photographie'. The contemporary film theorist Nicole Brenez recalls that 'la collection grise', as it was called, was an 'exceptional locus of theorisation' in the early 1980s.[22]

19   See Thierry Kuntzel, 'Le Travail du film', in *Communications*, n°23, cited earlier. See also Raymond Bellour, 'Thierry Kuntzel and the Return of Writing', in *Between-the-Images*, pp. 30–61.

20   See Roland Barthes, 'Le Troisième sens', in *L'Obvie et l'obtus* (Paris: Seuil, 1982), pp. 43–61. This essay originally appeared in *Cahiers du cinéma*, n°222 (July 1970), in a dossier on Eisenstein.

21   See Jean Narboni, *La Nuit sera noire et blanche: Barthes,* La Chambre claire, *le cinéma* (Paris: Capricci/Les Prairies ordinaires, 2015).

22   Nicole Brenez, 'The ultimate journey: remarks on contemporary theory', <http://www.screeningthepast.com/2014/12/the-ultimate-journey-remarks-on-contemporary-theory/>.

Indeed swiftly following Barthes' work were key publications by Pascal Bonitzer (*Le Champ aveugle*), Claude Ollier (*Souvenirs-écran*), Noël Burch (*Pour un observateur lointain*), Serge Daney (*La Rampe*) and Jean-Louis Schefer (*L'Homme ordinaire du cinema*). Schefer and Bonitzer's works were themselves, I would suggest, books 'in the wake' of *La Chambre claire*, Bonitzer's through its title (see later), and Schefer's because of the affective mode of the author's response to cinema and through the inclusion of photogrammatic stills, to which Schefer responds in the fragmentary mode characteristic of Barthes' later texts.[23] As Brenez remarks, the books in Narboni's collection would also 'irrigate' the theoretical monument of the decade, Deleuze's books *Cinéma I and II*, and this is partially borne out by a glance at the footnotes of *L'Image-mouvement* and *L'Image-temps*. *La Chambre claire*, however, is significantly lacking from Deleuze's frame of reference, although Deleuze will in his lectures at Vincennes consider Barthes' 'The Third Meaning' and 'Diderot, Brecht, Eisenstein', and in particular the thesis in the former that the essence of the filmic lies in the photogram, a proposition which he finds problematic.[24] This can be explained by a basic opposition – Barthes' work is focused on the still and on the detail of the photogram; for Deleuze the essence of cinema is in movement and in time.

It is this opposition that I aim to trouble in what follows, or to show that Barthes' text troubles. I think it is possible to read *La Chambre claire* perversely as a book which concerns cinema, or in which cinema is a concern, in part because of the context of its publication, but also because the oppositions Barthes sets up between photography and the cinema can be shown to be unstable, and to be scrambled within the logic of the text itself. I hope to show this, at least partially, in three stages.

Firstly, the assertion at the beginning of *La Chambre claire*: 'Je décrétai que j'aimais la Photo *contre* le cinéma, dont je n'arrivais pas cependant à la séparer' [I *decreed* that I liked Photography *against* Cinema, from which

---

23   See Jean-Louis Schefer, *L'Homme ordinaire du cinéma* (Paris: Cahiers du cinéma/ Gallimard, 1980).

24   Gilles Deleuze, Lecture of 29th January 1985, <http://www2.univ-paris8.fr/ deleuze/article.php3?id_article=299>.

I nevertheless could not separate it].[25] The preference for Photography is driven by a response to Cinema: Photography against Cinema. It makes sense to say, in Bazinian mode, that Cinema cannot be separated from Photography, due to the ontological relation the image has to its referent (which Barthes mentions on the very same page), and the fact that the Cinema consists, materially, of photogrammatic frames. But to be unable to separate Photography from Cinema as Barthes puts it here is to propose the latter as the starting point. *La Chambre claire* thus follows the proposition of 'The Third Meaning' that the essence of the filmic is in the photogram.[26] To this extent, and since Barthes does not have a theory of the difference between the photograph and the photogram, *La Chambre claire* extends the project of 'The Third Meaning' and the analysis of photograms; all of the images included in the text, and those discussed but not included, can be seen as *stills of a lost film*.

Secondly, the question of *movement*, of animation. English allows us to make a fairly facile pun around the *moving* image; the image in which there is movement, and the image which moves me, emotively. This is less easy in French, but Barthes will nevertheless exploit the confusion of literal and metaphorical and thus blur the distinction between the moving and the still image, a distinction which is nevertheless absolutely essential to the argument of *La Chambre claire*. Following a quotation from Sartre's *L'Imaginaire* about photographs which do not succeed in taking place 'for me', and leave me existentially indifferent, Barthes writes: 'Dans ce désert morose, telle photo, tout d'un coup, m'arrive; elle m'anime et je l'anime. C'est donc ainsi que je dois nommer l'attrait qui la fait exister: une *anima-tion*. La photo elle-même n'est en rien animée (je ne crois pas aux photos "vivantes") mais elle m'anime: c'est ce que fait toute aventure' [In this glum desert, suddenly a specific photograph reaches me; it animates me, and I animate it. So that is how I must name the attraction which makes it exist: an *animation*. The photograph itself is in no way animated (I do not believe in 'lifelike' photographs), but it animates me: this is what creates every

25   Roland Barthes, *La Chambre claire* (Paris: Cahiers du cinéma/Seuil, 1980), p. 13; trans. by Richard Howard (adapted), *Camera Lucida: Reflections on Photography* (New York: Hill and Wang, 1981), p. 3.
26   Barthes, 'Le Troisième sens', pp. 59–60.

adventure].[27] Movement is shifted here from the side of the object, so to speak, to the side of the subject; the image is not moving, but it makes me move, it moves me, animates me. The agency is in part on the side of the image – the image arrives, 'advenes', it happens 'to me', but the animation also depends, as the parenthesis suggests, on *belief*, and here we have a first intimation of a displacement that will be crucial for Barthes' response to and theorisation of images, moving or otherwise. They exist only in so far *as I believe in them* – affective investment, belief and ontology are made causally dependent. The distinction between movement and still, cinema and photography, is thus secondary to the distinction between those images which do not exist for me, because I believe in them, and those that don't, to which I am indifferent.

The third instance of this blurring of the distinction between photography and cinema concerns the issue of the 'blind field', where some terminological precision is necessary. I will cite at some length Barthes' remarks about this, which are a version of the argument proposed in *Roland Barthes by Roland Barthes* and in 'The Third Meaning', crudely, that I, 'R.B.', resist cinema because it is too fast, too much, too close.

> Dernière chose sur le *punctum*: qu'il soit cerné ou non, c'est un supplément: c'est ce que j'ajoute à la photo et *qui cependant y est déjà*. […] Est-ce qu'au cinéma j'ajoute à l'image? – Je ne le crois pas: je n'ai pas le temps: devant l'écran, je ne suis pas libre de fermer les yeux; sinon, les rouvrant, je ne retrouverais pas la même image; je suis astreint à une voracité continue: une foule d'autres qualités, mais pas de pensivité; d'où l'intérêt pour moi du photogramme. Pourtant, le cinéma a un pouvoir qu'à première vue la Photographie n'a pas: l'écran (a remarqué Bazin) n'est pas un cadre, mais un cache: le personnage qui en sort continue à vivre; un 'champ aveugle' double sans cesse la vision partielle. Or devant des milliers de photos, y compris celles qui possèdent un bon *studium*, je ne sens aucun champ aveugle: tout ce qui se passe à l'intérieur du cadre meurt absolument, ce cadre franchi. Lorsqu'on définit la Photo comme une image immobile, cela ne veut pas dire seulement que les personnages qu'elle représente ne bougent pas, cela veut dire qu'ils ne *sortent* pas: ils sont anesthésiés et fichés, comme des papillons. Cependant, dès qu'il y a *punctum*, un champ aveugle se crée (se devine).[28]

27   Barthes, *La Chambre claire*, p. 39; *Camera Lucida*, p. 20.
28   Barthes, *La Chambre claire*, pp. 89–90.

[Last thing about the *punctum*: whether or not it is triggered, it is an addition: it is what I add to the photograph and *what is nonetheless already there*. […] Do I add to the images in movies? I don't think so; I don't have the time: in front of the screen, I am not free to shut my eyes; otherwise, opening them again, I would not discover the same image; I am constrained to a continuous voracity; a host of other qualities, but not *pensiveness*; whence the interest, for me, of the photogram. Yet the cinema has a power which at first glance the Photograph does not have: the screen (as Bazin has remarked) is not a frame but a mask; the man or woman who emerges from it continues living, a 'blind field' constantly doubles our partial vision. Now, confronting millions of photographs, including those which have a good *studium*, I sense no blind field: everything which happens within the frame dies absolutely once this frame is passed beyond. When we define the Photograph as a motionless image, this does not mean only that the figures it represents do not move; it means that they do not *emerge*, do not *leave*: they are anesthetized and fastened down, like butterflies. Yet once there is a *punctum*, a blind field is created (is divined).][29]

Barthes looks back at the photos he has commented thus far – the Black woman with the round collar in the Van der See photograph has, for Barthes, a life outside the picture. He *wants to meet* Bob Wilson. He also proposes that the presence and dynamics of the 'champ aveugle' [blind field] are what distinguish the erotic photograph from the pornographic photograph. The latter immobilises sex and fetishises it, while the erotic photograph draws the spectator outside its frame. The *punctum*, then, Barthes proposes, is 'a subtle off-screen', and he adds, 'as if the image launched desire beyond what it permits us to see', towards 'the excellence of a being, body and soul together'.[30]

Before looking more closely at the notion of the 'champ aveugle' or the 'hors-champ' – which Barthes seems to use interchangeably here – I want to pause just to note again the importance of the noun *être*; 'l'excellence d'un être', and the logic of Barthes' argument: the *punctum* draws the spectator outside the frame – that is, in my interpretation, beyond the limits of the frame and *into* the virtual world of the *hors-champ*. In other words, the

29   Barthes, *Camera Lucida*, pp. 56–7.
30   'Le *punctum* est alors une sorte de hors-champ subtil, comme si l'image lançait le désir au-delà de ce qu'elle donne à voir: pas seulement vers "le reste" de la nudité, pas seulement vers le fantasme d'une pratique, mais vers l'excellence absolue d'un être, âme et corps mêlés' (Barthes, *La Chambre claire*, p. 93).

punctum draws or sucks the spectator *in* to the frame and across its borders, into the world which exists beyond those limits. It wounds and pricks precisely in opening this space up inside me for me to project myself into. And it draws the spectator in through the desire it instigates, a desire for a being, *un être*. Again, what seems to be at stake here, for me, is *a belief that the other exist*s, a desire for the other in their existence. It is a desire voiced in Rimbaud's expression 'posséder la vérité dans une âme et un corps' (to possess truth in body and soul).[31]

Barthes engages here, as he did also with the article on Cinemascope, with an already established film theory debate around the concept of the 'hors-champ'. The parameters of the debate were set by André Bazin in the essays of the 1940s and 1950s collected in *Qu'est-ce que le cinéma?* Barthes names Bazin here, but without giving a precise reference; he also omits any reference to Bazin in the list of references at the end of the book, despite the fact that its ontological orientation owes much to Bazin's famous and fundamental proposition of the 'ontological' nature of the photographic image. Colin McCabe finds this lack of a more explicit engagement with Bazin on Barthes' part 'absolutely extraordinary'; it is in part explained, one might think, by a fundamental difference in the respective arguments: for Bazin the ontological nature of the photographic image is merely extended in the cinema, which simply adds greater realism by adding movement to a medium impoverished by its absence; for Barthes, it seems, cinema obfuscates the ontological argument by the 'continuous voracity' with which it solicits my gaze.[32] However, one might also see the absence of reference here as a sign that Barthes wishes, intentionally or not, to cultivate a grey area around the notion of the 'hors-champ'. Margaret Iversen, in *Beyond Pleasure: Freud, Lacan, Barthes* notes that the implication that 'champ aveugle' is an expression from Bazin's discussion of the screen (given by the fact that Barthes puts the expression in inverted commas in the same

---

31   Arthur Rimbaud, 'Adieu', in *Une Saison en enfer*, *Œuvres complètes* (Paris: Gallimard, coll. Pléiade, 2009), p. 280.

32   Colin MacCabe, 'Barthes and Bazin: The Ontology of the Image', in Jean-Michel Rabaté (ed.), *Writing the Image after Roland Barthes*, p. 74.

sentence as the mention of Bazin) is erroneous.[33] Bazin does not use that
expression. The expression 'champ aveugle' thus seems to be an invention
of Barthes' own, one taken up by Pascal Bonitzer for the title of his 1982
contribution to the 'grey collection'. By substituting 'aveugle' for 'hors',
Barthes in effect again introduces a degree of ambivalence around the
limits between the still and the moving image. Even though you can't *see*
the off-screen world, Barthes intimates, this will not stop you believing in
it, believing that it exists and entering into it.

Barthes' 'slippage' – intentional or not – condenses an extended debate
around the 'hors-champ', launched by Bazin and persisting beyond Barthes'
intervention. It will be useful to resume, somewhat crudely, some of the
major points: Bazin distinguishes as Barthes says between the frame of
the painting or the stage of the theatre, which enclose and limit the world
within them, and the screen of the film, which acts as a 'mobile mask' – *un
cache* – delimiting a section, but only a section, of a world which extends
beyond the edges of the screen. This basic opposition – the cinematic screen
has a virtual off-screen world, painting and theatre do not, is extended by
Barthes to the opposition between photography and cinema. Noël Burch,
extending Bazin's model, offers a substantial and exhaustive classification of
all the different modes of the off-screen, organised according to the 'side'
of the screen, but he also adds the key distinction between the *concrete*
off-screen and the *imaginary* off-screen.[34] The concrete *hors-champ* is the
portion of the real which the camera could make visible, while the imaginary
off-screen is the whole background of context, history, psychology which
the spectator may be called upon to imagine in support of what they see.
Barthes' 'blind' field – not just what is not yet seen but what cannot be
seen, incorporates this distinction. Jean Mitry argues against Bazin, and
proposes that the notion of the off-screen can be applied to *any* image.[35]
Jacques Aumont proposes a useful summary of the various positions in his

33   Margaret Iversen, *Beyond Pleasure: Freud, Lacan, Barthes* (Philadelphia: Pennsyl-
     vania State University Press, 2007), p. 255.
34   Noël Burch, *Une praxis du cinéma* (Paris: Gallimard, 1986), especially chapter 2,
     ' "Nana" ou les deux espaces'.
35   Jean Mitry, *Esthétique et psychologie du cinéma* (Paris: Éditions Universitaires,
     1963–1965).

book *The Image*, but maintains the Bazinian principle that the *hors-champ* of the moving image can be revealed, while that of the still image can only ever be imagined.[36] In Pascal Bonitzer's writing on the question, however, we find the important qualification, against Burch, that there is no 'becoming field of the off-screen'; the off-screen is not only that which can be revealed, it is also that which is never revealed, which never becomes visible but always remains 'outside'; Barthes' *champ aveugle* – blind field – appears a prescient insight in this regard, rather than a careless misattribution.[37] The implication of this is that the 'hors-champ' of the film is always other than what is shown or what it might potentially show; there is always another world of the film, another film behind the film.[38]

Despite the dedication of *La Chambre claire* to Sartre's *L'Imaginaire*, or perhaps in keeping with it, given the arguments of the latter book, the capacity to *imagine* the world off-screen is not sufficient. Or at least Barthes does not use the vocabulary of imagination in reference to the world which the punctum endows with existence. He uses the lexis of existence and of belief. And here Gilles Deleuze's later discussion of the *hors-champ* becomes perversely pertinent. The question of *belief* enters into the picture, so to speak, of Deleuze's discussion of the 'hors-champ' in *L'Image-mouvement*. Drawing on Bazin, but also on Burch, Ollier, Mitry and Bonitzer, Deleuze develops a dualist theory of the *hors-champ* which again extends it beyond reference to the cinematic moving image alone, but also moves beyond the opposition between concrete and imaginary. The dualism in Deleuze's system lies between a *relative* relation between the space enclosed by the frame and a larger space one does not see: '[U]n aspect relatif par lequel un système clos renvoie dans l'espace à un ensemble qu'on ne voit pas, et qui peut être à son tour vu, quitte à susciter un nouvel ensemble non-vu,

---

36 Jacques Aumont, *L'Image* (Paris: Nathan, 1990).

37 Pascal Bonitzer, *Le Champ aveugle* (Paris: Gallimard/Seuil, 1982).

38 The concept of the *hors-champ* overlaps significantly with the notion of the 'travail du film' developed by Kuntzel – the film in the can has a plural textuality only partially (parsimoniously) realised in the projected film and can thus be considered as off-screen. It also overlaps with the more radical concept of 'acinéma' proposed by Lyotard in 'Acinéma', included in Jean-François Lyotard, *Des Dispositifs pulsionnels* (Paris: Galilée, 1994).

à l'infini' [A relative aspect by means of which a closed system refers in space to a set which is not seen and which can, in turn, be seen, even if this gives rise to a new unseen set, on to infinity], and an absolute relation between what one sees, and another, radically other order: '[U]n aspect absolu par lequel le système clos s'ouvre à une durée immanente au tout de l'univers, qui n'est plus un ensemble et n'est pas de l'ordre du visible' [an absolute aspect by which the closed system opens onto a duration which is immanent to the whole universe, which is no longer a set and does not belong to the order of the visible].[39] Further on Deleuze will qualify this second, more 'disturbing' *hors-champ* as 'a more radical Elsewhere, outside homogenous space and time', and propose that in cases where the relation between the visible world and the world around it, in other words in films in which the visible portion of the world is particularly restricted, the other function of the hors-champ is realised more profoundly, which is to 'introduce the trans-spatial and the spiritual into the system which is never perfectly closed'.[40]

Barthes does not quite subscribe, I would argue, to the quasi-vitalist philosophy that Deleuze articulates here as elsewhere throughout his work; however the idea outlined here, of an hors-champ qualified as *spiritual* resonates with the notion of the *champ aveugle* which Barthes proposes in *La Chambre claire*, for which it is not a question of a potentially visible section of the world that might be revealed to me through the camera's movement, or through montage and narrative progression, but of a spiritual investment, a sense of belief in the lives of the beings pictured in the photographs. The *hors-champ*, for Barthes, is the domain of the vitality of the photographed being, which his desire drives him to believe in. Barthes' look is evaluative and desiring, conditioned by the availability of the body (thus the 'adventure' in Barthes' sense, of the image of Robert Maplethorpe's outstretched arm and hand, which has just the right degree of *availability – disponibilité*). According to this measure, all images (can) have their off-screen, and the formal distinction between the still and the moving image recedes into the

39   Gilles Deleuze, *Cinéma I: L'Image-mouvement* (Paris: Minuit, 1985), p. 30; *Cinema 1: The Movement-Image*, trans. by Hugh Tomlinson and Barbara Habberjam (London: Athlone, 1986), p. 17.
40   *Ibid.*

background in relation to the determining force of the evaluative, desiring and spiritual aspects of the look.

To Enter Madly into the Image

This theoretical background amply supports my second example – Barthes' encounter with the sequence of the dance with the automaton Rosalba in Fellini's 1976 film *Casanova*, which occurs in the penultimate 'chapter' of *La Chambre claire*, titled 'La Folie, la Pitié' [Madness, Pity] in the 'Table of Contents' at the end of the volume.[41] The previous chapter had ended with the issue of the 'truth of madness', with a reference to a volume of essays convened by Julia Kristeva from her seminar of 1979, *Folle vérité* (Mad Truth). Barthes' point, leading on from that chapter, is that the 'noeme' – the defining essence – of photography approaches madness in almost, madly, reaching that point at which the intensity of affect becomes a guarantee of existence; the truth of the image or of desire causes a 'mad' belief that it exists, a form of hallucination. The madness is also there, Barthes argues, in the strange 'evidence' of photography. If the image, he says, is the negation of the object, and thus can tell us nothing about the existence of the object, the Photograph is a *new class* of image which 'proves', through its chemical magic, the existence of the object, that it *was*. The photograph is thus a kind of hallucination – an image which is felt as a real perception – thus a 'mad' image which has been as if

41   Gordon Hughes interprets Barthes' comments on the sequence from Fellini's *Casanova* as a 'reference within a reference', to Hoffman's 'The Sandman' and through it to Freud's essay 'The Uncanny'. These resonances are striking – Barthes writes as we will see of his eyes being struck by an 'atrocious acuity', echoing the threat that the Sandman will come and steal the eyes of Nathaniel, and later Nathaniel will fall in love with the automaton Olympia. Hughes deploys this parallel to indicate the 'indeterminacy' common to the uncanny and to photography; we are not sure if we are dealing with the real or with a hallucination. See Gordon Hughes, '*Camera Lucida*, circa 1980', in Gregory Batchen (ed.), *Photography Degree Zero: Reflections on Roland Barthes' Camera Lucida* (Cambridge, MA: MIT Press, 2009).

'rubbed up against' the real.[42] Barthes is concerned here with the crossing over and intermixing of different categories – that of ontology, perception, the order of the image and the order of the affect. The encounter with photograph, as an encounter with the real, and the hallucinatory confusion of *having existed* with *existing*, but also the tragic confusion of affective intensity ('I loved') with proven pastness ('she was and is no more') comes close to the kind of psychosis that is at stake in Kristeva's psychoanalytic investigations in *Folle vérité*. These considerations introduce an anecdote which Barthes intends as an exemplification or a specification perhaps of the kind of hallucination that is at stake.

On the evening of a day on which he had looked again (not for the first time, then) at the photographs of his mother (so not just the Jardin d'Hiver photograph), he went with some friends to see Fellini's *Casanova* at the cinema. In a madeleine-like episode, amidst the irritating spectacle, an epiphany arises:

> J'essaye de rendre la spécialité de cette hallucination, et je trouve ceci: le soir même d'un jour où j'avais encore regardé les photos de ma mère, j'allai voir, avec des amis, le *Casanova* de Fellini; j'étais triste, le film m'ennuyait; mais lorsque Casanova s'est mis à danser avec la jeune automate, mes yeux ont été touchés d'une sorte d'acuité atroce et délicieuse, comme si je ressentais tout d'un coup les effets d'une drogue étrange; chaque détail, que je voyais avec précision, le savourant, si je puis dire, jusqu'au bout de lui-même, me bouleversait: la minceur, la ténuité de la silhouette, comme s'il n'y avait qu'un *peu* de corps sous la robe aplatie; les gants fripés de filoselle blanche; le léger ridicule (mais qui me touchait) du plumet de la coiffure, ce visage peint et cependant individuel, innocent: quelque chose de désespérément inerte et cependant de disponible, d'offert, d'aimant, selon un mouvement angélique de 'bonne volonté'.[43]

> [I am trying to render the special quality of this hallucination, and I find this: the same evening of a day I had again been looking at photographs of my mother, I went to see Fellini's *Casanova* with some friends; I was sad, the film exasperated me; but when Casanova began dancing with the young automaton, my eyes were touched with a kind of painful and delicious intensity, as if I were suddenly experiencing the effects of a strange drug; each detail, which I was seeing so exactly, savouring it, so to speak, down to its last evidence, overwhelmed me: the figure's slenderness, its tenuity – as if there were only a trifling body under the flattened gown; the frayed

---

42   'frottée de réel' (Barthes, *La Chambre claire*, p. 177).
43   Barthes, *La Chambre claire*, p. 179.

gloves of white floss silk; the faint (though touching) absurdity of ostrich feathers in the hair, that painted yet individual, innocent face: something desperately inert and yet available, offered, affectionate, according to an angelic impulse of 'good will'.][44]

Previously Barthes has said that the film proceeds or processes ('défile') too quickly for him to be able to *think* it; he has thus had recourse to stills to be able to allow the image to come out to him, to wound him. Here, it is as if the film slows down while processing normally, or as if his perception were suddenly slowing down, as if he were able in his 'ordinary' viewing to still and slow the film so as to take in each of the *puncta* offered to him. The *pensiveness* of the image, its *champ aveugle* too, does not then depend on the formal stillness of the image, but on another stillness, or another form of movement.

What makes this possible? It is, Barthes proposes, a combination, a knot in fact, of madness and some other affect which he begins to call love, but specifies as Pity.

> N'étais-je pas, en somme, amoureux de l'automate fellinien? [...] Pourtant, ce n'était pas tout à fait ça. C'était une vague plus ample que le sentiment amoureux. [...] une autre musique se faisait entendre, au nom bizarrement démodé: la Pitié.

> [Was I not, in fact, in love with the Fellini automaton? [...] Yet it was not quite that. It was a broader current than a lover's sentiment. In the love stirred by Photography (by certain photographs), another music is heard, its name oddly old-fashioned: Pity.][45]

Fellini's automaton gives Barthes an image which correlates with the noeme of Photography – which itself had been given to him by the Winter Garden Photograph, from which he had derived all photography. It is not just that 'it has been' (*ça a été*), but something that obliges him to believe, madly, that he can, he must, enter into the image:

> Je rassemblais dans une dernière pensée les images qui m'avaient 'point' (puisque telle est l'action du *punctum*), comme celle de la négresse au mince collier, aux souliers à brides. A travers chacune d'elles, infailliblement, je passais outre la réalité de la chose représentée, *j'entrais follement dans le spectacle, dans l'image*, entourant de mes bras

---

44 Barthes, *Camera Lucida*, p. 115.
45 *Ibid.*

ce qui est mort et ce qui va mourir, comme le fit Nietzsche, lorsque le 3 janvier 1889, il se jeta en pleurant au cou d'un cheval martyrisé: devenu fou pour cause de Pitié.[46]

[I collected in a last thought the images which had 'pricked' me (since this is the action of the *punctum*), like that of the black woman with the gold necklace and the strapped pumps. In each of them, inescapably, I passed beyond the unreality of the thing represented, I entered crazily into the spectacle, into the image, taking into my arms what is dead, what is going to die, as Nietzsche did when, as Podach tells us, on January 3, 1889, he threw himself in tears on the neck of a beaten horse: gone mad for Pity's sake].[47]

What justifies the parallel between the Winter Garden photograph and the Fellini automaton sequence? Is it more than a parallel? Perhaps a bleeding of affect, as if the Fellini sequence resonates affectively, sparks the memory of looking at the photographs of his mother like a screen memory? In both instances we are concerned with the body of a woman. Perhaps, again as a kind of screen memory, Barthes transfers into his relation with Fellini's automaton the grief he felt for his dead mother, which seems also to linger in Nadar's photograph of his mother, reproduced in the text some pages earlier. What this evokes in him is the desire to take the body in his arms, a desire Barthes transfers again, through the reference to Nietzsche's 'mad' act of Pity with the Turin Horse. The body of the automaton, like that of Barthes' mother, is 'disponible' (available), not for sex, though Casanova will indulge this, but for tenderness and love. Barthes notes that the feeling is wider ('plus ample') than love, since it involves, it seems, the embrace – that is, the physical contact, but also the acceptance – of 'that which is dead and will die'. These words, which Barthes had employed with reference to Lewis Payne, and metonymically transferred to his recently deceased mother, and to the beings of all those photographs which had 'wounded' him. The essence of Photography ends up being the Pity/Tenderness which affects the living when confronted with the image of mortality.

The point is perhaps that the automaton, an uncanny double between life and death, is animated but not. It brings into play a whole set

46   Barthes, *La Chambre claire*, p. 179.
47   Barthes, *Camera Lucida*, p. 116.

of associations around the still and the moving image, a realm of ambivalence that Barthes seems already to have dismissed too swiftly in 'decreeing' his preference for Photography against cinema. Fellini's automaton offers Barthes a sequence-image which captures the possibility and the necessity of belief, the 'mad' belief in the possibility of 'entering into' the spectacle, as if in revolt against death, to return in time in order to save the one you love from death.

Barthes' encounter with the Fellini sequence will count among the 'moments of Truth' that he identifies in the Collège de France lecture course in 1979, contemporaneous with the composition of *La Chambre claire*. It is a crucial element in the elaboration, in the lecture course, of an 'evaluative' and affective theory of both reading and writing, formulated around the 'moments of truth' such as this. This offers us, beyond orthodox notions of literary theory, the programme for a future research:

> Critique pathétique: au lieu de partir d'unités logiques (analyse structurale), on partirait d'éléments affectifs → on pourrait aller jusqu'à une discrimination des valeurs (de la valeur) de l'œuvre selon la *force* des moments – ou d'un moment: tout le *Casanova* de Fellini (que je n'aime guère) sauvé parce que l'automate a fait tilt en moi.

> [Pathos critique: instead of starting from logical units (structural analysis), we would start from affective elements → we could go as far as a discrimination of the values (the value) of the work according to the *force* of the moments or of a moment: the whole of Fellini's *Casanova* (which I don't like much) saved because the automaton pricked me].[48]

Barthes elaborates here the basis for a theory of literary affect, which he specifically distinguishes from the structural analysis he had previously favoured. My contention has been that the *force* and the *truth* of the text are tied to the capacity to believe, to hallucinate an existence outside living presence.

48   Barthes, *La Préparation du roman I et II*, p. 160.

PART II

On Pleasure, Fatigue and Death in/of the Text

Textual Exhaustion and Oscillations

KOHEI KUWADA

3 Pleasure and Fatigue of the Barthesian Text

As is well known, Roland Barthes began to emphasise the importance of pleasure explicitly in his work at the beginning of the 1970s. After suggesting the possibility of a hedonistic aesthetics in 'From Work to Text' (1971)[1] – an aesthetics that depends on the pleasure of the reader, considered not as a consumer but as a producer of the text – Barthes developed this hedonistic aesthetics further in *The Pleasure of the Text* (1973). In the last chapter of the book, the concept of 'writing aloud' is presented as an example of the 'aesthetics of textual pleasure'. Barthes seems to consider that whether a piece of writing speaks aloud or not depends on readers' ears being sufficiently sensitive and attentive. While relying on a distinction between the pheno-text and the geno-text taken from the work of Julia Kristeva, Barthes focuses on the material or physical dimensions of writing at the expense of its meaning and message:

> Due allowance being made for the sounds of the language, *writing aloud* is not phono-
> logical but phonetic; its aim is not the clarity of messages, the theater of emotions;
> what it searches for (in a perspective of bliss) are the pulsional incidents, the language
> lined with flesh, a text where we can hear the grain of the throat, the patina of con-
> sonants, the voluptuousness of vowels, a whole carnal stereophony: the articulation
> of the body, of the tongue, not that of meaning, of language.[2]

1   Roland Barthes, 'De l'œuvre au texte' [1971], in *Œuvres complètes*, ed. by Éric Marty (Paris: Seuil, 2002), vol. III, pp. 908–16; 'From Work to Text', in *The Rustle of Language*, trans. by Richard Howard (New York: Hill and Wang, 1986), pp. 56–64.
2   Roland Barthes, *The Pleasure of the Text*, trans. by Richard Miller (New York: Hill and Wang, 1975), pp. 66–7. Unless otherwise stated, the italics are in the original text.

It cannot be overlooked that he declares that 'writing aloud is not phonological but phonetic'. Far from being a logic (*logos*), this aesthetics of pleasure forces us to listen to what occurs in the text, or more precisely, to every sound that the text *is producing* in each reading. Barthes conceives the notion of the text by making an analogy to a body *in vivo*, such that the pleasure of the text could arise from the encounter and exchanges between two singular bodies: that is, the (textual) body of the author and the body of the reader. Thus, with the notion of the pleasure of the text, Barthes invites us to sharpen our sensitivity to the sensuous body of the author that emerges in a text. It is not the theory of pleasure but the resonance of senses that matters here. This short essay proposes to listen carefully to the sounds his own *body* raises unwittingly when Barthes talks *aloud* about pleasure. And by doing so, we will bring to light an inseparable and intricate connection between pleasure and fatigue in the writings and thought of Roland Barthes, even if these two terms seem opposed at first glance.

In order to better understand the notion of pleasure for Barthes, it is worth examining two quotations from *Roland Barthes by Roland Barthes* (1975). The first one is concerned with his fragmentary way of writing and shows clearly why he is a hedonist:

> Liking to find, to write *beginnings*, he [Roland Barthes] tends to multiply this pleasure: that is why he writes fragments: so many fragments, so many beginnings, so many pleasures (but he doesn't like the ends: the risk of the rhetorical clausule is too great: the fear of not being able to resist the *last word*).[3]

We ought to note that pleasure always goes hand in hand with fear for Barthes, as *The Pleasure of the Text* begins with an epigraph from Hobbes: 'La seule passion de ma vie a été la peur' (My one passion in life has been fear).[4] Thus, without being immersed in the euphoric atmosphere that this fragment could create, we will have to examine his confession in

3   Roland Barthes, *Roland Barthes by Roland Barthes*, trans. by Richard Howard (Berkeley/Los Angeles: University of California Press, 1977), p. 94.

4   Roland Barthes, *Le Plaisir du Texte* [1973] in *Œuvres complètes*, ed. by Éric Marty (Paris: Seuil, 2002), vol. IV, p. 217; *The Pleasure of the Text*, p. xi. The English translator decided to reproduce the exact quotation from Hobbes's original Latin text instead of translating the Barthes's quotation (in French) into English.

the parenthesis in relation to his conception of pleasure. Let us not forget that he had already mentioned the '[p]roximity (identity?) of bliss and fear'[5] in a different perspective. We should not take the image of Barthes as a hedonist too literally. As becomes clear from reading his books, to 'resist the last word' is a strategy to defend his own singularity (and of course that of others), preventing any reduction of himself (and of others) to an object or a simple image. Here you can see his ethical and political intentions: 'The "private life" is nothing but that zone of space, of time, where I am not an image, an object. It is my *political* right to be a subject which I must protect.'[6] If Barthes takes pleasure each time in writing a beginning, it is because he believes he can multiply himself or his images by writing as many beginnings as possible. This is the characteristically Barthesian form of engagement, which aims not only to defend the political right to his own singularity, but also not to define others, especially his friends, as objects. This ethical attitude was called 'morality' in *Roland Barthes by Roland Barthes*. He considers in this auto-fiction that his works since *The Pleasure of the Text* belong to the genre of 'morality', which he cannot, however, conceptualise. In a fragment entitled 'Friends', Barthes attempts to clarify this notion of 'morality' that can be considered, according to him, as a flexible network of friendships where every friend obtains, day by day, his or her own identity and originality through the conversations between them. In this context, any identity is precarious and ceaselessly recomposed, like a text 'which will never come to an end'.[7] As a result, his resistance against the last word is intended to increase the bonds of friendship through a variety of pleasures: so many fragments, so many beginnings, so many pleasures … and so many friendships. It is therefore his ethical and political engagement that logically caused the praise of pleasure, and not the reverse.

The specific character of Barthesian engagement is fully manifested in the second quotation:

5   Barthes, *The Pleasure of the Text*, p. 48.
6   Roland Barthes, *Camera Lucida: Reflections on Photography*, trans. by Richard Howard (New York: Farrar, Straus and Giroux, 1981), p. 15.
7   Barthes, *Roland Barthes by Roland Barthes*, p. 64.

Suppose that the intellectual's (or the writer's) historical function, today, is to maintain and to emphasize the *decomposition* of bourgeois consciousness. Then the image
must retain all its precision; this means that we deliberately pretend to remain within
this consciousness and that we will proceed to dismantle it, to weaken it, to break
it down on the spot, as we would do with a lump of sugar by steeping it in water.[8]

Being different from Sartrean engagement, which aims to protest
against social conditions *by means of* a certain language, Barthes has gone
as far as protesting against language itself, which is inevitably soaked in
bourgeois ideology (the doxa, public opinion, stereotype) because our
culture is, in his opinion, entirely bourgeois. Hence his famous strategy of
'cheating (with) language'.[9] Barthes is perfectly aware that he is more or less
on the side of his opponent insofar as there is nothing beyond or outside of
the bourgeois culture. The obvious allusion to the famous words of Henri
Bergson ('If I want to mix a glass of sugar and water, I must, willy-nilly,
wait until the sugar melts')[10] underlines the importance of waiting that
is naturally imposed by Barthesian engagement. In order to promote the
decomposition of bourgeois consciousness, which is also that of Barthes
himself, he should avoid attacking it frontally in the hope of getting immediate results, but instead wait patiently until it collapses immanently
and gradually. Barthesian engagement takes time to show its first effects.
And it makes him tired. His fatigue increases while waiting since his own
consciousness is dismantled more and more. Barthes declares: '[t]he stereotype can be evaluated in terms of *fatigue*. The stereotype is what *begins* to
fatigue me.'[11] It is not only the stereotype but also its deconstruction that
fatigues him. We should therefore admit the coexistence of two Barthes: a
hedonist Barthes who delights in multiplying beginnings and pleasures as
much as possible, and a Barthes tired from his constant efforts to prevent
the last word, which can all too easily be stereotypical. So many fragments,

8   *Ibid.*, p. 63.
9   Roland Barthes, 'Inaugural Lecture, Collège de France', in *A Barthes Reader*, ed.
      by Susan Sontag (New York: Hill and Wang, 1982), p. 462 (translation slightly
      modified).
10   Henri Bergson, *Creative Evolution*, trans. by Arthur Mitchell (London: Macmillan,
      1922), p. 10.
11   Barthes, *Roland Barthes by Roland Barthes*, p. 89.

so many beginnings, so many pleasures, so many friendships … and so many fatigues. It might seem evident that the work of Barthes becomes increasingly a-political and a-historical for advocating pleasure at all cost, especially from *The Pleasure of the Text* onward. But once one recognises Barthes's fatigue, the following analysis seems inescapable:

> In any case, even the flight from history and politics is a reaction to those realities and a way of registering their omnipresence, and the immense merit of Barthes' essay is to restore a certain politically symbolic value to the experience of *jouissance*, making it impossible to read the latter except as a response to a political and histor-ical dilemma, whatever position one chooses (puritanism/hedonism) to take about that response itself.[12]

The praise of pleasure at the expense of politics and history reinforces, paradoxically, and in accordance with the psychoanalytic notion of 'denial', a political and historical dilemma. In the 1950s and 1960s, Barthes engaged in a series of reflections on politics and history by demystifying various social stereotypes. Probably discouraged and tired by this painful work of demystification, Barthes decided to advocate a return to pleasure in the early 1970s. But the more clearly he takes a hedonistic attitude by talking aloud about the importance of pleasure, the more we can feel his fatigue from the inevitable constraint of politics and history. Pleasure and fatigue are therefore inseparably linked in Barthes's writing.

Barthes must have felt such fatigue throughout his life. He was always tired of defending his own singularity, that of his friends, and that of his beloved mother against generality, gregariousness, or stereotype. Without taking into account and even sharing such fatigue, one cannot understand what he meant by 'pleasure'. Consequently, writing on Roland Barthes, we cannot but feel, in our turn, the same fatigue as he had felt, because we run the same risk of reducing Barthes to an image or an object – and therefore of contravening his principle of 'morality'. There is always a great difficulty in writing directly on Roland Barthes. We may have to invent an indirect way of writing on him, a way to see him obliquely. Éric Marty is therefore

---

12   Fredric Jameson, *The Ideologies of Theory. Essays 1971–1986, vol. 2: Syntax of History* (London: Routledge, 1988), p. 69.

not wrong to simply write his personal memories and impressions in order to 'restore a presence, a voice, an existence which are not his own'.[13] Marty made a choice to write on Roland Barthes by not speaking directly of the latter. It would not be enough merely to recognise an intimate relationship between his notion of pleasure and his fatigue. It is more important to share and sympathise with his fatigue; otherwise we would not feel the sensuous body of the author that emerges in a text, that is, the pleasure of his text. In his lecture course on the Neutral given at the Collège de France in 1977–8, Barthes himself associates fatigue with his literary work, referring to Maurice Blanchot: 'I use its infiniteness as an accompaniment of my work. Here, one grasps this: fatigue: in one sense, the opposite of death, since death – the unthinkable definitive ≠ fatigue, the infinitude but livable in the body.'[14] We can conclude that it is the dialectical movement between fatigue and pleasure that determines Barthes's writing and that allows him to keep on writing.

13   Éric Marty, *Roland Barthes, le métier d'écrire* (Paris: Seuil, 2006), p. 13 (my translation).
14   Roland Barthes, *The Neutral: Lecture Course at the College de France (1977–1978)*, trans. by Rosalind Krauss and Denis Hollier (New York: Columbia University Press, 2007), p. 20.

FUHITO ENDO

4 Genealogy of Textual Necrophilia or Death Drive Barthes, Freud, De Man and Mehlman[1]

Barthes and Freud

Roland Barthes's *The Pleasure of the Text* is implicitly fascinated with the impossible textuality of Sigmund Freud's *Beyond the Pleasure Principle*, to the extent that the former is thematically and linguistically haunted by the latter.[2] Worth remembering is that the meta-psychology in Freud's text is a struggle to theorise the unpleasure of pleasure or the pleasure of unpleasure, where this chiasma deconstructs Freud's speculations on primal masochism or 'the death drive'. I would argue that what Barthes admits as the 'ambiguity' in his terminology of 'pleasure' (*plaisir*) and 'bliss' (*jouissance*) is a trace of his fascination with the Freudian chiasma of pleasure/unpleasure.[3] It is well established in the critical discourse that unpleasure in Freudian psychoanalysis is something 'beyond the pleasure principle' – the biological principle that 'unpleasure corresponds to an

---

1   This argument was revised in Japanese with particular reference to affect theories as a chapter of my monograph-length book: *Jyoudou to Modernity* [Affect and Modernity] (Tokyo: Sairyusha, 2017).

2   Several comparisons have been made between Barthes and Freud from the viewpoint of the death drive. See, for example, Margret Iversen, *Beyond Pleasure: Freud, Lacan, Barthes* (University Park: Pennsylvania State University Press, 2007). However, these comparisons have not so far given due attention to Freud's radical contradictions in his meta-psychology on the death drive and Barthes's fascination with them, crucial to the discussion in this chapter.

3   Roland Barthes, *The Pleasure of the Text*, trans. Richard Miller (New York: Hill and Wang, 1975), p. 19. All references hereafter given in parentheses in the text.

increase in the quantity of excitation and pleasure to a *diminution*'.⁴ Freud's clinical encounter with traumatic war neuroses, however, provided him with a daunting or rather blinding insight into the radical paradox inherent in his own definition of pleasure, where 'the patient is […] fixed to his trauma' (13). Hence, Freudian neurosis as a fixation or a recurring and persistent attachment to trauma, the cause of the illness, and the maximum degree of excitation/unpleasure. Another implication is that a Freudian neurotic *enjoys* the unpleasure of excessive excitation through his/her repetitive fixation precisely in the sense that Freudian unpleasure is 'beyond' but at the same time *within* pleasure. This is the real connotation of the title of Freud's paper *Beyond the Pleasure Principle*.

In this connection, worth citing in full is Roland Barthes's fascination with the ambiguity in his own use of 'pleasure'/'bliss'. He writes:

> *Pleasure of the text, text of pleasure*: these expressions are ambiguous because French has no word that simultaneously covers pleasure (contentment) and bliss (rapture). Therefore, 'pleasure' here (and without our being able to anticipate) sometimes extends to bliss, sometimes is opposed to it. But I must accommodate myself to this ambiguity; for on the one hand I need a general 'pleasure' whenever I must refer to an excess of the text, to what in it exceeds any (social) function and any (structural) functioning; and on the other hand I need a particular 'pleasure', a simple part of Pleasure as a whole, whenever I need to distinguish euphoria, fulfillment, comfort (the feeling of repletion when culture penetrates freely), from shock, disturbance, even loss, which are proper to ecstasy, to bliss. I cannot avoid the fact that in French 'pleasure' refers both to a generality (*'pleasure principle'*) and to a miniaturization (*'Fools are put on earth for our minor pleasures'*). Thus I must allow the utterance of my text to proceed in contradiction. (19–20)

Of crucial importance in the discussion is what Barthes implies by the word 'bliss' (rapture) or *jouissance*. There is no doubt that he connects this conception with something masochistic, the pleasure of displeasure. As a matter of fact, this word is indicative of 'shock, disturbance, even loss' in contrast to 'fulfilment' or 'comfort' (which exactly corresponds

---

4   Sigmund Freud, 'Beyond the Pleasure Principle', in *The Standard Edition of the Complete Psychological Works of Sigmund Freud*, vol. XVIII (London: Hogarth, 1955), pp. 1–64 (p. 8). All references hereafter given in parentheses in the text. Unless otherwise noted, all emphases in this chapter are from the original texts.

to Freud's 'pleasure principle'). Elsewhere in the text, Barthes's 'bliss' expresses a clearer connotation of masochism: 'Text of bliss: the text that imposes a state of loss, the text that discomforts' (14). In the above block quotation, on the other hand, Barthes's pleasure has to do with 'an excess of the text', which suggests some intensity of linguistic excitation. The suggestion is that Barthesian bliss/pleasure is an ecstatic/rapturous enjoyment of something uncomfortable (disturbing) and even excessive and traumatic (shocking). Thus his 'ambiguity' of pleasure/bliss is far more complicated and contradictory than we tend to assume. His 'bliss' appears at once within *and* beyond the semantic register of 'pleasure' in a manner similar to the way Freudian displeasure is within *and* beyond the semantic category of pleasure. This perspective motivates the consideration that Barthes's fascination with Freudian masochistic/chiasmic illogic privileges the 'Text of bliss' which 'unsettles the reader's historical, cultural, psychological assumptions' and even 'brings to a crisis his relation with language' (14).

No less intriguingly, this Freudian 'uncanny (*unheimlich*)' ontology of Barthes's pleasure/bliss ambiguity – or bliss within/without pleasure and *vice versa* – can be viewed as relevant to another textual/linguistic 'crisis' – contradiction. Let us remember Barthes's 'ecstatic' resignation: 'Thus I must allow the utterance of my text to proceed in contradiction.' From the very beginning, Barthesian *bliss*ful references to '*logical contradiction*', '*illogicality*', '*incongruity*', or '*self-contradiction*' are obvious (3). He honours an 'anti-hero', or rather a kind of anti-Christ who *endures/enjoys* a Biblical 'punishment'. As he explains:

> [W]ho endures contradiction without shame? Now this anti-hero exists: he is the reader of the text at the moment he takes pleasure. Thus the Biblical myth is reversed, the confusion of tongues is no longer a punishment, the subject gains access to bliss by the cohabitation of languages *working side by side*: the text of pleasure is a sanctioned Babel. (3–4; emphases added)

Rhetorically speaking, Barthes's obsession with something contradictory or confused/confusing is connected with a set of spatial metaphors including 'breaks' (6), 'seam' (7), 'tear' (10), 'hole' or 'gap' (12), 'split' and 'cleavage' (47).

Of special interest is the way in which a textual divisiveness represented by these figures reveals itself as 'the place where the death of language is glimpsed' (6). What distinguishes Barthesian textual masochism from others that conform to 'the reader's historical, cultural, psychological assumptions' is not its radical refusal to enjoy the displeasure of mere death or destruction; but rather that he is *enraptured* with the logical impossibility of such death/destruction. For example, one possible definition of textual 'modernity' given by Barthes is as follows:

> Whence, perhaps, a means of evaluating the works of our modernity: their value would proceed from their duplicity. By which it must be understood that they always have two edges. The subversive edge may seem privileged because it is the edge of violence; but it is not violence which affects pleasure, nor is it destruction which interests it; what pleasure wants is the site of a loss, the seam, the cut, the deflation, the *dissolve* which seizes the subject in the midst of bliss. (7)

Barthes, in this context, mentions 'Sade's libertine' who 'manages to be hanged and then to cut the rope at the very moment of his orgasm, his bliss' in quest of something 'untenable, impossible' (7). The 'duplicity' here is thus suggestive of the simultaneity – or at-the-very-same-moment-ness – of the maximum and zero degree of bliss/death. This is a logical (for that matter, biological) impossibility – 'the cohabitation of languages *working side by side*', or the coexistence of maximum and zero degrees – as a certain kind of materialisation of textual dividedness (seam, tear, hole, gap). As such, Barthesian bliss, as the impossible, manifests itself 'in the form of a pure materiality' (7). This materiality is the impossible 'site of a loss' for the simultaneity of the maximum/zero degree of the text. Roland Barthes, in *Writing Degree Zero*, is more explicit as to the impossibility of sexuality/textuality of modernity: 'For Literature is like phosphorous: it shines with maximum brilliance at the moment when it attempts to die.' By definition, '[m]odernism begins with the search for a Literature which is no longer possible' (38). Barthes regards such impossible textuality/ sexuality as symptomatic of a certain sort of neurosis. As he describes:

> Neurosis is a makeshift: not with regard to 'health' but with regard to the 'impossible' Bataille speaks of ('Neurosis is the fearful apprehension of an ultimate impossible', etc.); but this makeshift is the only one that allows for writing (and reading). (5)

This textual neurosis once again motivates us to read Barthes and Freud side by side, while visualising an invisible dialogue between Barthes, Freud *and* Paul de Man as well, another 'neurotic' critic who is rapturously preoccupied with the impossible possibility of textual lethality.

Freud and de Man[5]

Despite the apparent lack of Paul de Man's sympathy with psychoanalysis, there are a set of intriguing and unexpected affinities between the two authors. As Shoshana Felman recollects in her essay 'Postal Survival, or The Question of the Navel', de Man 'shunned' psychoanalysis.[6] Felman is quite right in suggesting that de Man 'resisted the discourse of psychoanalysis. And yet, he resisted it as one who was extremely close to it, as one who in a way knew all about it' (51–2). Her focus is thus on 'a complex dialogue with psychoanalysis' or 'a lifelong dialogue engaged [...] between de Man's emotional proximity to, and simultaneous critical distance from, the psychoanalytic discourse' (52). Curiously enough, in this context, de Man wrote to Felman just before his death, giving some comments on her essay on psychoanalysis. He pays particular attention to the 'navel' in Freud's *Interpretation of Dreams*: something that de Man sees as the 'mark, which separates as much as it unites' (68). Inspired by de Man's concern about the navel – the paradoxical place embodying 'at once the *disconnection* and the *connection* between a maternal body giving birth and a newborn child' (63) – Felman argues:

5   Part of this section is based on my paper 'The Material Event of the Death Drive: Freud and De Man Reconsidered', presented at the 111th *Annual Conference of the Pacific Ancient and Modern Language Association* (San Diego, 13 November 2013).

6   Shoshana Felman, 'Postal Survival, or The Question of the Navel', *Yale French Studies*, n°69 (1985), pp. 49–72 (p. 57). All references hereafter given in parentheses in the text.

> Unlike Freud, whose image of the navel as a knot seems to convey the wish to *go inside*, to plunge *into* the unknown, de Man's vision of the knot conveys the wish – or the necessity – of *getting out* of an entrapment. For Freud, the navel is a '*point of contact* with the unknown': Freud is looking for the continuity of the paradoxical figure of discontinuity, for the connection of the disconnection. De Man, in contrast, insists on the discontinuity disrupting the continuity, on the disconnection of the connection. (71)

The navel – as a paradoxical site of connection and/or *dis*connection – itself thus *at once* connects and disconnects de Man and Freud. In addition, Felman points out that de Man is interested in 'the manifest bisexuality' (68) of the navel, and her discussion focuses largely on the sexual and gender implications of the navel's paradoxical status. Taking a cue from Felman's essay, I argue that de Man's rather unusual expression of his interest in something psychoanalytic and Freudian – in this case 'the navel' – implies something more. By which I mean that this paradoxical simultaneity of connection and disconnection is a crucial topic in my comparison of de Man, Freud and Barthes.

Given de Man's interest in or obsession with the impossible and deconstructive simultaneity of opposites, it is evident that the Freudian navel has much to do with de Manian deconstruction. We need to remember that – semantically speaking – the navel in Freudian dream texts is a site or place that means too much to mean anything. This is indeed the semantics of what Freud calls 'over-determination (*Überdeterminierung*)'. His navel in a dream text can be over-determined simultaneously by a number of mutually contradictory, unconscious representations to represent anything specific on its manifest level. Semantically speaking, then, it is too 'condensed' to mean anything. In other words, it is at once within and beyond the semantics of Freudian dream texts. From the viewpoint of psychoanalytic semantics, this may be read as the simultaneity, *at-the-same-time-ness*, or short-circuit of the maximum and zero degree of representational and semantic intensity. The Freudian navel means too much to mean anything, and is thus a textual product of the impossible and simultaneous materialisation of two extremes in its semantic system. The polarity in this semantics – its maximum and zero degrees – are at once radically disconnected *and* connected with each other in Freudian dreamwork.

Worth mentioning in this context is Andrzey Warminski's views on de Manian textual materiality – or what he terms a 'material event' – in his 'Pascal's Allegory of Persuasion'. Particularly important is the manner in which 'the zero' as a trope – or an impossible trope – 'disrupts Pascal's geometric epistemological discourse' just because the zero '*signifies* too much (and too little) to be a sign; it *designates* too much (and too little) to be a trope.'[7] Of course, it is in the Freudian dream text that this kind of impossible simultaneity of radically incompatible things – the semantic maximum and zero degree – materialises itself as the navel, which indeed – as de Man himself suggests – 'separates as much as it unites' those opposite semantic extremes.

Significantly, this semantic impossibility shares a great deal with Freud's meta-psychological speculations on the death drive. To summarise the difficulty of Freud's position, it can be said that the impossible simultaneity of the maximum and zero degree of libidinal energy or excitation manifests or physicalises itself in the symptom of the death drive as a repetition compulsion. As Freud himself admits, the death drive is 'the most obscure and inaccessible region of the mind' (7) impossibly divided by a paradox – the repetitive, compulsive and masochistic drive to obtain 'an *increase* in the quantity of excitation' (8) and *at the same time* to 'return to the quiescence of the inorganic world' (62). It is a drive which simultaneously moves towards the maximum *and/but/or* zero degree of libidinal intensity. In *The Pleasure of the Text*, Barthes remarks: 'repetition itself creates bliss'; 'to repeat excessively is to enter into loss, into the zero of the signified' (41). This is amply suggestive of the libidinal paradox of the death drive, in which the excessiveness/displeasure is connected and disconnected with the libidinal or semantic zero/pleasure.

'Pascal's Allegory of Persuasion' thus again foregrounds the textual affinities between de Man and Freud. De Man's depiction of Pascal's textual predicament is worth quoting at length. He writes:

---

7   Andrzej Warminski, 'Introduction: Allegories of Reference', in Paul de Man, *Aesthetic Ideology*, ed. by Andrzej Warminski (Minneapolis: University of Minnesota Press, 1996), pp. 1–33 (pp. 29–30).

The situation is not only unstable, but *coercive* as well. At this point, one moves from the logic of proposition, statements as to what is the case, to modal logic, statements of what should or ought to be the case. For one cannot remain suspended between the irreconcilable positions: it is clear that, by not choosing between the two poles of the polarities, one is adopting the skeptical position. The predicament is that of the undecidable: propositional logic is powerless to decide a conflict that has to find a solution, if this logic is to survive.[8]

These two kinds of textual logic – propositional and modal – develop de Man's speech act theory. He claims that: '[p]ropositional statements line up on the side of cognition, modal statements on the side of performance; they perform what they enunciate regardless of considerations of truth and falsehood.' De Man stresses that this textual performance exerts 'pure coercive power' (68) as it were *beyond* the philosophical principle of true or false. What characterises or drives Pascal's texts is therefore 'a function of the heterogeneity between cognitive and performative language'. De Man continues:

> Language, in Pascal, now separates in two distinct directions: a cognitive function that is right but powerless, and a modal function that is mighty in its claim to rightness. The two functions are radically heterogeneous to each other. (69)

At the cognitive and philosophical level of Pascal's language, it is suspended or divided between 'the two poles of the polarities' – or what we have so far termed 'two radically incompatible things'. At the very same time, his language is urged or driven by some performative/coercive intensity – what de Man calls 'sheer quantitative power' – beyond the philosophical principle. At a mathematical and philosophical level, his language is not able to 'square, to inscribe the four terms *présence/absence* and *plaisir/déplaisir* [note the similarity] into a homogeneous "geometrical structure"' (69). Paul de Man's concluding sentence is interesting in terms of his definition of 'allegory': 'The (ironic) pseudoknowledge of this impossibility, which pretends to order sequentially, in

8   Paul de Man, 'Pascal's Allegory of Persuasion', in *Aesthetic Ideology*, ed. by Andrzej Warminski (Minneapolis: University of Minnesota Press, 1996), pp. 51–69 (p. 64). All references hereafter given in parentheses in the text.

a narrative, what is actually the destruction of all sequence, is what we call allegory' (69). De Manian 'allegory' can thus be read as a forced self-destructiveness or dividedness of the text despite its own self-conscious resistance against it.[9]

Pascal's textual plight is reminiscent of Freud, especially *Beyond the Pleasure Principle*. Just like Pascal, at the cognitive or psychological level, this text is quite 'powerless' in managing its logical and theoretical contradictions. As we have seen, Freud's death drive itself is a paradoxical connection and disconnection of the opposites – the maximum and zero degree of libidinal intensity. Significantly, what characterises Freud's text is also 'the heterogeneity' between its cognitive and performative discourses. At the cognitive level, it is filled with indeterminacy; however, by way of contrast, the text's performance is powerful in its persistence as a meta-psychological argument. In his reading of Pascal, de Man regards the cognitive level as 'the language of truth and of persuasion by proof', and the latter performative dimension as 'the language of pleasure' (69).

To continue this intertextual comparison of the texts in question, a crucial aspect of Freud's meta-psychology, especially in *Beyond the Pleasure Principle*, is a foregrounding of masochism in his speculations on the death drive. According to Freud's pleasure principle, a decrease of libidinal excitation means pleasure and a corresponding increase in displeasure. As we have observed, if one possible definition of the death drive is a desire to obtain an 'increase in libidinal excitation', then it should be defined as a drive to enjoy displeasure. In *The Freudian Body*, Leo Bersani explains just how the masochistic aspect of the death drive forms or *de*forms the performance of *Beyond the Pleasure Principle* as a textual body.[10] Freud's

9   A complete examination of de Man's highly nuanced and charged meanings of the term 'allegory' is beyond the scope of this argument. For further consideration of this word, see Andrzej Warminski, ' "As the Poets Do It": On the Material Sublime', in *Material Events: Paul de Man and the Afterlife of Theory*, ed. by Tom Cohen et al. (Minneapolis: University of Minnesota Press, 2001), p. 3–31. Also useful are Warminski's more recent works, *Material Inscriptions: Rhetorical Reading in Practice and Theory* (Edinburgh: Edinburgh University Press, 2013) and *Ideology, Rhetoric, Aesthetics: For de Man* (Edinburgh: Edinburgh University Press, 2013).

10 See Leo Bersani, *Freudian Body: Psychoanalysis and Art* (New York: Columbia University Press, 1986).

meta-psychological speculations are fatally flawed by the logical disruption of the chiasmic juxtaposition of pleasure and/or displeasure. On the
cognitive level, Freud is at the mercy of this radical paradox; at the same
time, his language never relinquishes its meta-psychological projects despite
or rather because of its theoretical impossibility. This textual persistence
or impossible endeavour is an embodiment of its masochistic enjoyment
of theoretical collapse as 'self-shuttering' (3): hence the Freudian *Body*.
Just like Freud's neurotic patients, his text itself enjoys its self-destructive
bodily compulsion.

In this manner, in *Beyond the Pleasure Principle*, de Man's coercive 'language of pleasure' *enjoys* its own meta-psychological self-destruction. This
is what Bersani sees as a Freudian textual and masochistic performance.
Freud's text is forced to enjoy the displeasure of its own cognitive disruption. This could be considered as a self-reflexive/destructive performance
of its own meta-psychology on the death drive. From de Man's reading of
Pascal, therefore, Freud's meta-psychology could be read as 'the pseudoknowledge of this impossibility'. Indeed, Freud's psychoanalysis, 'which
pretends to order sequentially, in a narrative, what is actually the destruction of all sequence, is what we call allegory'. The de Manian 'allegory'
thus shares a good deal with Barthes's 'Text of bliss', which is a struggle to
'restore within science what goes against it: here, the text' (33). Without
doubt, *Beyond the Pleasure Principle* is a 'Text of bliss' in the Barthesian
sense – a meta-psychological, self-destructive project to restore within
psychoanalysis what goes against it.

Given this perspective, in the midst of the Barthesian pleasure of
textual displeasure/dividedness, we can find 'the cohabitation of languages
working side by side' (perhaps the language of truth and the language of
pleasure). Consequently, since 'the death of language is glimpsed' here,
this indicates a genealogy of *textual necrophilia*, shared by Barthes, Freud
and de Man. They are readers who endure/enjoy textual contradictions
and radical dividedness – a lethal impossibility or impossible lethality as
the simultaneity of a maximum/zero degree of libidinal/textual semantics.

Mehlman/Barthes[11]

The political connotation of Barthesian textual pleasure/bliss is quite revolutionary. As Barthes explains:

> No significance (no bliss) can occur, I am convinced, in a mass culture (to be distinguished, like fire from water, from the culture of the masses), for the model of this culture is petit bourgeois. It is characteristic of our (historical) contradiction that significance (bliss) has taken refuge in an excessive alternative: either in a mandarin *praxis* (result of an *extenuation* of bourgeois culture), or else in an utopian idea (the idea of a future culture, resulting from a *radical, unheard-of, unpredictable* revolution, about which anyone writing today knows only one thing: that, like Moses, he will not cross over into it). (38–9)

This dialectic of bourgeois/revolutionary extends our genealogy of textual necrophilia to another critic who also shares a preoccupation with the impossible simultaneity of the representational – both textually and politically – maximum/zero degree: Jeffrey Mehlman, especially in his *Revolution and Repetition: Marx/Hugo/Balzac.*[12] Of crucial significance is that Mehlman regards Marx's Bonapartism, which is represented or rather misrepresented in his *The Eighteenth Brumaire of Louis Bonaparte*, as the traumatic textual excesses of Marx's dialectic of the bourgeoisie and the proletariat, thereby marking 'a break with the notion of class representation' (14) in Marxian terms. Marx's rhetoric in this text foregrounds his

---

11   Part of this section is based on my article 'The Death Drive of Revolution/Counter-Revolution', *(a): The Journal of Culture and the Unconscious* (Special Issue: The Freudian Left Reconsidered, The California Psychoanalytic Circle), vol. 8, n°1 (2012), pp. 63–72. It is interesting to note that Mehlman worked with de Man at Yale and de Man's praise of Mehlman's book is cited on the back cover. This suggests their shared interest in the textual 'perversity' of Freud. Given the contemporariness of their publications – including Barthes's work mentioned in this chapter – their genealogical similarity is representative of highly rich and sophisticated readings of Freud's death drive especially from the late 1970s to the early 1980s.

12   Jeffrey Mehlman, *Revolution and Repetition: Marx/Hugo/Balzac* (Berkeley: University of California Press, 1977). All references hereafter given in parentheses in the text.

dialectic as the thematic dichotomy of surface, higher, bourgeoisie versus depth, lower, proletariat, while at the same time suggesting that this high and low dialectical structure collapses or is 'frozen' as Mehlman explains (13). What collapses or freezes is the *lumpen-proletariat* as something excessive or uncontainable, some uncanny *matter* or *Thing* in and out of this historical class system. Mehlman depicts the *lumpen-proletariat* as 'something lower than the low' as follows:

> For it is as though the movement of dialectic had been frozen. Whereas the *higher* was inevitably to be overthrown by the *lower* – the bourgeoisie by the proletariat – those two poles remain constant and are mutually impoverished by a strange irruption of *something* lower than the low … at the top. (13)

> We would suggest at this juncture that for Marx as writer, *The Eighteenth Brumaire* is above all the site where that heterogeneity, in its unassimilability to every dialectical totalization, is *affirmed*. (13)

> For from the very beginning of our inquiry, we have continuously encountered in – and with – Marx's text the repetitive insistence of a specific structure: the irruption of a *third* element which in its heterogeneity, asymmetry, and unexpectedness, breaks the unity of two specular terms and rots away their *closure*. In – or rather, outside – the class struggle, against Marx's expectation, we observe the *lumpen-proletariat* irrupting at the summit of society. (19)

This 'movement' of 'dialectical totalization' is driven by the structure in which 'the low' as a dialectical negativity is subsumed within 'the higher', thereby the former negating and simultaneously reforming or refining the latter: a positivity. In Mehlman's words, '[t]he negativity which gnaws at and motivates history is utterly subordinate to an invincible positivity' (9).

What subverts this textbook dialectic is another structure in which a Marxian 'negation of negation' – 'something lower than the low' – does not contribute to this dialectical process or reproduction; rather, the Marxian dialectic is 'frozen' or 'collapsed' by this more *radical* negativity. More importantly, this radical negativity as a negation of negation refuses to be contained within the reformed or refined 'positivity' in the form of a dialectical *Aufhebung*. Instead, this negation of negation – 'something lower than the low' – is absolutely and materially 'affirmed' as it is, in spite or because of its sheer negativity, thus paralysing the Marxian dialectical totalisation. This radical and *material* negativity is thus *at once* negated *and* affirmed; ontologically and topologically speaking, it is both within (affirmed) and out of (negated) Marx's representation of the class struggle.

This paradoxical ontological status of the radical negativity as the *lumpen-proletariat* – 'something lower than the low' and at the very same time 'the summit of society' – in Marx's class dialectic, provides it with a certain type of textual intensity or unique materiality. Quoting from Marx's rhetoric, Mehlman describes this as follows:

> For Bonaparte seems to short-circuit both dialectic and class struggle in gathering in his service the 'scum (*Auswurf*), offal (*Abfall*), refuse (*Abhub*) of all classes', the '*lumpen-proletariat*'. (13)

It is here that '[a] certain proliferating energy is thus released within Marx's writing upon contact with the Bonapartist instance', while making the author abuse it with 'almost Rabelaisian verve' (13) and relegate it to 'a scandal in history' (14) and 'the residues of class society, the *lumpen dejecta* of the class struggle' (38). Quite significant and intriguing is Marx's excessively Rabelaisian/alliterative way – *Auswurf, Abfall* and *Abhub* – of abusing and *enjoying* what may be termed 'the *lumpen* ex-crement'. In other words, negating *and* affirming, or rather absolutely affirming through radical negation, Marx abhors *and* enjoys the excessive residue or excretion of his historiography. What I would call a 'Rabelaisian scatological *jouissance*' of this kind leads us to read in Marx's text a unique sort of encounter with dung/*das Ding*. This is a Marxian textual materiality or intensity of what we could term the absolute affirmation of radical negativity. Mehlman is therefore right in saying: 'the *matter* of materialism [...] finds its precise point of insertion in Marx's text in the *excesses* of the Bonapartists' (23). This Marxian *matter* is simultaneously in *and* out of his theory of social classes. Bonapartism is by definition something scandalously uncanny that haunts/frustrates/fascinates Marx's history of class and revolution. Of course, we can discern here a striking similarity between Marx's *matter* and Barthes's 'pure materiality', both of which – as we have discussed – reveal themselves in the midst of textual

disconnection/connection of semantic or discursive maximisation (absolute affirmation) *and* zero degree (radical negation).

No wonder, then, that what Mehlman tries to highlight in this context
is the 'sinister anonymity' (5) of Marx's *The Eighteenth Brumaire of Louis
Bonaparte* and Freud's *The Interpretation of Dreams*. Mehlman's attempt is
to read the almost uncanny intertextuality – or intertwistedness – between
those texts. Based on this comparison, Mehlman depicts Bonapartism as
'the heterogeneous instance – in which is condensed a maximum of "dreamwork", of "unconscious", of "the repressed"' (40). Melman's implication is
that there is a significant affinity between Marx's failure in his class dialectic
and the failure of Freudian dreamwork. Put simply, Marx's class-based dialectic, or idea of class representation fails in much the same manner that
Freud's dream text fails. Worthy of special attention is Mehlman's emphasis
on 'what Marx call the "hieroglyph" of Bonapartism', when his text 'implicitly' works 'against the pertinence of the concept of representation' (18).
Marx's 'hieroglyph' – which connotes something unreadable and incompre-
hensible – tempts us to associate it with the 'navel' of Freudian dream texts.

To reiterate, what is implied here is that the maximum degree of
Freudian dreamwork or Marxian political representation produces something unreadable as Freud's navel and Marx's hieroglyph. This means that
the maximum degree of representational power – as both *Vertretung* and
Darstellung – simultaneously and automatically brings about something
radically unreadable or ineffable – the degree zero of its semantics and
politics. Marx's hieroglyph and Freud's navel can thus be seen as an embodiment or uncanny materialisation of the maximum *and* zero degree
of their representational power at the same time. In this connection, it is
useful to mention Kojin Karatani's reading of the paradoxical representational status of Louis Bonaparte. Karatani discusses one of the essential
scandals concerning Bonaparte: the fact, on which he insists, that he 'seizes
power as someone representing everyone' while 'maintain[ing] no necessary
link to the "represented"'.[13] Karatani's point is the arbitrary semiotic link
between signifier and signified. This linguistic arbitrariness is relevant to

13   Kojin Karatani, *History and Repetition*, ed. by Seiji M. Lippit (New York: Columbia
      University Press, 2003), p. 10 and p. 12.

our discussion. Bonaparte, as a signifier, represents everybody/nobody. It is precisely in this sense that he is a scandalous incarnation of Bonapartism as the simultaneity of the maximum/zero degree of the modern European representational system.

This semantic/political paradox leads Mehlman to suggest another uncanny parallel between Bonapartism and the Paris Commune. What repeats itself as the scandal, hieroglyph, or navel in Marx's representation – or rather misrepresentation – of history is thus the paradox of Bonapartism and the radical indeterminacy of revolution and counter-revolution. Indeed, this indeterminacy or uncanny sameness of opposites – in this case, revolution and counter-revolution – exasperates and enraptures Marx's language. In the language of Jeffrey Mehlman, the parallel between Bonapartism and the Paris Commune manifests itself as follows:

> [W]e may intuit the devious path joining 'the Bonapartist state' and 'the Commune', rendering them superimposable as the sites of a common heterogeneity in what we would call the Marxian fantasmatic. (38)

No doubt, Mehlman's views are 'marked by an experience of Freud at his most provocative', absorbed in 'the perversity of the repetition compulsion in two of its most striking formulations: "the uncanny (*das Unheimliche*)" and the "death drive"' (3).

This uncanny and chiasmic indeterminacy of Bonapartism/the Commune or revolution/counter-revolution invokes the Barthesian 'ambiguity' of pleasure/bliss. As discussed, the latter concerns the 'coexistence' or commingling of bourgeois 'comfort' or 'pleasure principle' *and* something 'disturbing', 'shocking' or suggestive of 'a *radical, unheard-of, unpredictable* revolution'. Just like Marx, the Barthesian reader is someone who enjoys/abhors this uncanny and chiasmic indeterminacy. Furthermore, the Barthesian uncanny or 'ambiguous' textuality of pleasure/bliss is strongly indicative of a genealogical affinity to Mehlman's thesis on *das Unheimliche*. As the American thinker explains:

> For one might well evolve the following thesis from the text on the uncanny: what is *unheimlich* about the *unheimlich* is that absolutely *anything* can be *unheimlich*. The term *anything* is eloquent with arbitrariness and impropriety; it suggests that what is

electively available to contamination by the *unheimlich* would seem so fundamentally
extrinsic to it as to be designated as its other: *Heimlichkeit*. (6–7)

This view is what I would term the semantic promiscuity of the uncanny –
the chiasmus or reversibility of radical opposites – whose 'arbitrariness
and impropriety' materialises itself as 'the perversity of the repetition
compulsion in two of its most striking formulations: "the uncanny (*das
Unheimliche*)" and the "death drive"'. I argue that such perversity bears
an intriguing relevance to what Barthes calls 'pure materiality' in the 'gap'
of which 'the death of language is glimpsed'. This is an *impossibly* scandalous textual place which attracts *and* disgusts (once again the opposites
are reversible here) Barthes, Freud, de Man and Mehlman. Thus emerges
the genealogy of textual necrophilia, where they all endure *and* enjoy 'a
certain collapse of the very possibility of metalanguage' (Mehlman, 7),
thereby disclosing their self-referential/destructive *jouissance* of the death
drive. Their textual sexuality is thus 'perverted' to the extreme degree of
enjoying and enduring the lethal impossibility/impossible lethality of the
at-the-same-time-ness of the maximum/zero degree of the text. This is
indeed the kind of 'site for loss' which dissolves into 'sinister anonymity'
the proper names 'Barthes', 'Freud', 'de Man' and 'Mehlman'.

5 Tragicomic Pleasure and Tickling-Teasing Oscillation in John Marston's *Antonio* Plays

The source of delight springing from the 'tragicomic' is a puzzle with no easy solution. It works with elements from both comedy and tragedy, frequently highlighting rather than downplaying incongruity. Incongruity has itself been seen as a trigger for the comic.[1] Paul Lewis sees 'humour as one of three primary responses to incongruity – the other two being curiosity and fear'.[2] The tragicomic seems however to play upon all three chords. Alenka Zupančič claims of 'the genre of tragicomedy' that it 'takes place within the tragic paradigm' and is 'tragedy's comedy', 'essentially a subgenre, or even a successor, of tragedy'.[3] Giambattista Guarini, in contrast, identified tragicomedy as taking from 'comedy' 'its happy reversals, and above all the comic order'.[4] This chapter, however, focuses on tragicomedy as striking instead a delicate balance between genres, drawing upon both, often keeping both in sight. Its peculiar pleasure springs from its edgy (and double-edged) instability and uncertainty – a precarious combination, already leaning towards excess on either side. Focusing on John Marston's *Antonio* plays (c.1600), parodic revenge tragicomedies written for the Children of Paul's boy-actor company,

---

1 See Immanuel Kant, *Critique of Judgement*, trans. by James Creed Meredith, ed. by Nicholas Walker (Oxford: Oxford University Press, 2007), p. 161.

2 Paul Lewis, *Comic Effects: Interdisciplinary Approaches to Humor in Literature* (Albany: State University of New York Press, 1989), p. x.

3 Alenka Zupančič, *The Odd One In: On Comedy* (Cambridge, MA: MIT Press, 2008), pp. 175–6.

4 Giambattista Guarini, 'Compendio della Poesia Tragicomica', trans. by Damiano Pietropaulo, in *Sources of Dramatic Theory*, ed. by Michael J. Sidnall (Cambridge: Cambridge University Press, 1991), p. 153.

this chapter will consider the pleasure derived from the comic dimension and that derived from the tragic. Particular attention will be given
to the tempering of both in the 'tragicomic' interplay – which modifies
both and produces a particular 'teasing' pleasure of its own, through
parody and the evasion of catharsis.

Genre Hybridity

The tragicomic as 'hermaphrodite of genres'[5] is a hybrid form, or a mode
between genres, possessing instability which endows it with capacity to
reveal the limits of both tragedy and comedy – the latter genre distinction already muddied by 'impurities' and instabilities in the Early Modern
period, as noted by Samuel Johnson in his critical prefaces to Shakespeare,[6]
as well as by George Steiner, who contrasts it with a more classical purity
of distinction.[7] Tragicomedy, in accentuating 'improper' juxtapositions,
has particular propensity for parody. Parody in the *Antonio* plays has
previously been read as working in both directions – Allen Bergson sees
Marston's *Antonio* plays as parodying 'romantic comedy',[8] while Philip
J. Ayres[9] suggests they bear a parodic intent in relation to Kydian revenge
tragedy.[10] However, in both accounts, parody seems dislocated from

5   Martin Wiggins, *Shakespeare and the Drama of His Time* (Oxford: Oxford
     University Press, 2000), p. 102.
6   Samuel Johnson, 'The Plays of William Shakespeare', in *The Major Works*, ed. by
     Donald Greene (Oxford: Oxford University Press, 1984), pp. 419–66 (p. 429).
7   George Steiner, *The Death of Tragedy* (New Haven, CT: Yale University Press,
     1996), p. 24.
8   Allen Bergson, 'Dramatic Style as Parody in Marston's Antonio and Mellida',
     Studies in English Literature, 1500–1900, vol. 11, n°2 (1971), pp. 307–25 (p. 307).
9   See Philip J. Ayres, 'Marston's *Antonio's Revenge*: The Morality of the Revenging
     Hero', *Studies in English Literature, 1500–1900*, vol. 12, n°2 (1972), pp. 359–74.
10   Thomas Kyd's *The Spanish Tragedy* (c.1586) – despite not being the first play to
     tackle such themes, as Wiggins points out (*Shakespeare and the Drama of His Time*,
     p. 33) – is considered to be the first major work to popularise revenge tragedy
     on stage.

comedy, with emphases on technique and critique which downplay the comic element. The crucial question for our purposes here is whether there is something specific about the pleasure arising from the tragicomic, in relation to the interplay between genres and attendant parody – which latter, I maintain, must always have something of the comic about it.[11]

The duality and in-betweenness of the tragicomic are explored in relation to Marston's *Antonio* plays, chosen because they make the inter-genre duality structurally manifest through intertextual links and incongruities, pointedly unfolding over two plays: *Antonio and Mellida*[12] and *Antonio's Revenge.*[13] Martin Wiggins comments on a further duality in the audience's response to tragicomedy, as a source of pleasure: its 'pleasure is two-fold: at one level we are engaged with the characters, live with them through their sufferings […] but at another we are enjoying the literary spectacle of a playwright deftly overcoming all obstacles'.[14] The response elicited by tragicomedy, double-layered as it is, is not an unproblematic engagement, but rather, one tempered by critical distance and awareness of the playwright's craft.

Metatheatricality and Metafiction

The metatheatrical dimension is an almost constant feature in the tragicomic mode, while the metafictional dimension tends to accompany parody.[15] This provides one means of generating critical (and comical)

11 Following Margaret Rose's definition of 'parody' as 'the comic refunctioning of pre-formed linguistic or artistic material' (*Parody: Ancient, Modern, and Post-Modern* (Cambridge: Cambridge University Press, 1993), p. 52).

12 John Marston, *Antonio and Mellida: The First Part*, ed. by G. K. Hunter (London: Edward Arnold, 1965). Further references to the play (hereafter *AM*) will be to this edition.

13 John Marston, *Antonio's Revenge*, ed. by Reavley Gair (Manchester: Manchester University Press, 1978). Further references to the play (hereafter *AR*) will be to this edition.

14 Wiggins, *Shakespeare and the Drama of His Time*, p. 120.

15 See Linda Hutcheon, *A Theory of Parody: The Teachings of Twentieth-Century Art Forms* (New York: Methuen, 1985).

distance from the action, sometimes framing affect as affectation, while forging another avenue of pleasurable engagement in an additional understanding and awareness partially shared with the reader/audience. In tragicomedy, the metatheatrical may provide a margin for *play* and parodic commentary, opening up the space for the potential of re-accentuation that could alter the balance between constituent genres. Audience response is difficult to gauge in view of the plays' meagre recent production history (on the few occasions they have been performed, they have tended to be separated – such as the production of the second part by Edward's Boys, in 2011). I therefore here discuss audience expectations, where relevant, as contingent upon theatrical tradition (particularly when foregrounded as significant within the play-text) and genre patterns.

The scripted Induction to *Antonio and Mellida* establishes metatheatricality as a concern before the play officially 'opens'. The Induction is a 'paratextual'-threshold device[16] which serves as an introduction, and a sort of extended prologue with actors' commentary. In this case, it would seem to require the viewer to submit to a split and duality in vision, and keep in sight performer and role/character, 'impossibly' and necessarily occupying the same space, in simultaneity. The actors appear in various degrees of 'characterisation' and discuss their parts in an exchange scripted and fashioned to appear 'improvised' – thus, while it makes us aware of the metatheatrical dimension in relation to the plays, the 'behind the scenes' glimpse seems to offer another kind of informal intimacy. The Induction highlights the incompleteness of the usurpation and displacement of actor by role, stressing the boy-actors' deficiencies. Alberto advises the actor playing Piero to 'grow big in thought/As swoll'n with glory', in order to fill the stately proportions of the 'adult' role scripted for a boy (*AM*, Induction 11–2).

Metatheatrical tragicomedy seems to allow the audience a stolen 'wink', as it were – the wink, as the mark *par excellence* of mischievous collusion,

---

16 A 'paratext' as defined by Genette includes presentational devices, titles, epigraphs, and all that surrounds and occurs alongside the 'main' body of text: 'More than a boundary or a sealed border, the paratext is, rather, a *threshold*' (Gérard Genette, *Paratexts: Thresholds of Interpretation*, trans. by Jane E. Lewin (Cambridge: Cambridge University Press, 2001), pp. 1–2).

of the metafictional – yet, always only one eye open, the other closed, as something is reserved in the promise of pleasure extended. Indeed, any Induction or Prologue is a threshold figure – perhaps physically closer to the audience, metatheatrically framing and occupying the space of incongruity – intensifying, therefore, both connection and disconnection from the central action. Metatheatrical highlighting of mimetic inadequacies (including the *Henry V* Chorus – 'Right ill-disposed in brawl ridiculous', IV. 0. 51),[17] if read literally, could provide grounds for a parodic version. Yet the *Henry V* Chorus, more consistently if not completely, retains his threshold properties, while a figure like Balurdo violates the sanctity of the *locus*, even during the play's main action.[18] Some of the actors in Marston's Induction have already half-entered their role – some comment on the process, others speak 'in character' – placing them on the threshold of a threshold. There is, in the lack of clear distinction, a space opened up for shifting emphases and re-accenting – a characteristic belonging more 'properly' to the 'impropriety' of the comic realm. It testifies to the instability of the mode of the 'tragicomic-parodic' – instability which demands the reader/viewer's adjustment and flexibility, exploring variations of pleasure in response.

[Inter]play

The first play, *Antonio and Mellida*, stages 'the comic crosses of true love' (V. 2. 265), with the eponymous lovers overcoming obstacles to finally unite, through complicated contrivances, and a series of disguises and

17   Shakespeare's *Henry V* Chorus both apologises for and celebrates the limitations of the 'swelling scene' (Prologue, 4).

18   I here make use of Robert Weimann's terms. The 'locus' is the area of the stage occupied by characters of a higher status, authority, or more integrally caught up in the action, while the *platea* is the threshold-area held by characters with a closer connection to the audience – of a lower status within the play, or having a role which includes commentary on the action. See Douglas Bruster and Robert Weimann, *Prologues to Shakespeare's Theatre: Performance and Liminality in Early Modern Drama* (London: Routledge, 2004), pp. 26–8.

misrecognitions – its happy resolution seems to be the end appropriate to a comedy, with general rejoicing and apparent restoration of order. A coffin as a stage device suggests the provisionality of stage-death, when Antonio rises from it to be reunited with his lover, invoking the protective mantle of comedy's foolery – that continued rebounding which enables comic repetition.[19] This enables the pleasure that springs from the continuing possibility of re-activation.

There is a perceptible shift in tone from *Antonio and Mellida* to *Antonio's Revenge*, signalled by the title of the latter (announcing it as a revenge play) and its wintry prologue: 'The rawish dank of clumsy winter ramps/The fluent summer's vein' (*AR*, Prologue 1–2). Therefore, the first play appears to prioritise the comic, while the second promises tragedy. Yet, the opposition is not so clear-cut. The promise of re-visiting in a sequel (a sequel to a comedy, furthermore) is more typically suited to parody's comic turn, which depends on some element of repetition.[20]

The interrelationship between the two plays is key to the peculiarity of the pleasure generated by its overall vision – which is not seamlessly unified. Seeming lack of coherence and cohesion between (as indeed, within) Marston's *Antonio* plays may appear puzzling,[21] yet there is something to be gained from considering them as a 'diptych', as Wiggins does.[22] The discontinuities emerging from their interrelationship are as important as the continuities. Repetitions and echoes between the plays include masques, disguises and false reports of Antonio's death. However, the shifts in tone

19   See Henri Bergson, 'Laughter', in *Comedy: 'An Essay on Comedy' by George Meredith, 'Laughter' by Henri Bergson*, ed. by Wylie Sypher (Baltimore: John Hopkins University Press, 1980), pp. 61–190.

20   See Mikhail Bakhtin, *Problems of Dostoevsky's Poetics*, ed. and trans. by Caryl Emerson (Minneapolis: University of Minnesota Press, 1984), p. 217; Gérard Genette, *Palimpsests: Literature in the Second Degree*, trans. by Channa Newman and Claude Doubinsky (Lincoln: University of Nebraska Press, 1997), p. 5.

21   'Marston's *Antonio* plays oscillate between tragic rhetoric and blatant face, moral *sententiae* and apparent self-parody. […] but I confess myself baffled as to what they are in themselves, he seems so little committed to the violence he presents' (Nicholas Brooke, *Horrid Laughter in Jacobean Tragedy* (London: Open Books, 1979), p. 6).

22   Wiggins, *Shakespeare and the Drama of His Time*, p. 103.

underlying these connections seem more calculated to cause discomfort, than unify. This 'pleasurable' discomfort is linked to the frustration of expected satisfaction, in the manner of foreplay which delays climax. Adam Phillips' analysis of foreplay and tickling as 'dependent' on the ability 'to hold [...] the experience' is relevant here:

> This means to stop at the blurred point, so acutely felt in tickling, at which pleasure becomes pain, and the [one tickled] experiences an intensely anguished confusion; because the tickling narrative, unlike the sexual narrative, has no climax.[23]

The threshold position of the plays is one of oscillation and continuous deferral of satisfaction: a tickling-teasing pleasure, even as the clamour of collisions and over-inflated 'play' dissipates into a series of 'false' endings.

The pervasive tonal inconsistencies, though they may indicate a 'design',[24] yet resist the kind of unifying reading put forward by Allen Bergson – indeed, such a reading tends to rely on the prioritisation of one play over the other, or of tragedy over comedy, to some extent suppressing the other – Allen Bergson sees *Antonio and Mellida* as 'prologue to *Antonio's Revenge*',[25] with parody reinforcing an ultimately tragic vision. Ayres' claims of 'consistency' in characterisation are almost wholly based on the second play.[26] Intertextual echoes within the plays, however, encourage us to maintain another duality of vision alongside the parodic: holding both plays in mind.

There is, moreover, a bridge which is also an intervening (unstaged) stage between the two plays – during which the violent death of Antonio's father Andrugio occurs. This originates in an old rivalry between the two fathers – Antonio's and Mellida's – which precedes the events of the first play. Andrugio haunts the second play, in 'theatrical' form, as an 'embodied' ghost. This double haunting, with its incongruity of the ghostly corporeal, highlights the superimposition of comic and tragic – co-existing

23   Adam Phillips, *On Kissing, Tickling, and Being Bored: Psychoanalytic Essays on the Unexamined Life* (Cambridge: Harvard University Press, 1993), p. 10.

24   Ayres, 'Marston's *Antonio's Revenge*', p. 373.

25   Allen Bergson, 'Dramatic Style as Parody in Marston's Antonio and Mellida', p. 324.

26   Ayres, 'Marston's *Antonio's Revenge*', p. 370.

and vacillating. Neither is unequivocally uppermost, neither attains complete fruition alone – prolonging the pleasure of 'foreplay'.

Relationships, parallels and exchanges between characters mirror the duality of structure and genre. Piero, Mellida's father and maniacal villain, finds himself jostled by various digressions in *Antonio and Mellida*, and in *Antonio's Revenge* the 'serious' attention he would claim is undermined by the courtier Balurdo's antics – as overtly comic foil – threatening to upstage him. The suspicion of everything being 'overdone' (*Hamlet*, III. 2. 18–9) leaves room for 'burlesque' interpretation, through excess, exaggeration and reflexive superfluity: 'It may be possible to imitate [the tragic hero], but then we shall be passing, whether consciously or not, from the tragic to the comic.'[27] Mechanical, exaggerated, inadequate imitation, rigidly observing trappings but not passionate sentiment, is proposed by Bergson as a source of comedy's pleasure, reminiscent of childhood games. This is the pleasure provoked by Balurdo's bombast-inflating aping of the self-important tragic villain Piero, which deflects the potentially tragic and noble into the 'comic'. The entrances of Balurdo fantastically dressed occur at inappropriate moments, most apt therefore for the maximal comic effect to be derived from contrast. Balurdo's child-like enthusiasm magnifies disproportion, and reasserts the value of 'play'.

Loose Ends and Untrustworthy Endings

A claim could be made for the tragicomic being a more all-encompassing vision: 'The tragic action, however inspiring [...] runs through only one arc of the full cycle of drama; for the entire ceremonial cycle is birth: struggle: death: resurrection. The tragic arc [stops at] death.'[28] Yet, the plays refuse such sweeping resolution of contradictions into a 'cycle' – manifesting rather a resistance which denies the *end* of pleasure. Antonio

27   Bergson, 'Laughter', p. 166.
28   Wylie Sypher (ed.), *Comedy: 'An Essay on Comedy' by George Meredith, 'Laughter' by Henri Bergson* (Baltimore: John Hopkins University Press, 1980), p. 220.

is believed dead, and lives. Indeed, 'impurities' persist, as something of the comic lingers in death, not always (though sometimes, with calculated arbitrariness) 'final'. Andrugio's ghost in *Antonio's Revenge*, aforementioned representative of the 'dead', bears the stamp of the actor's body. Death itself becomes an unreliable ending, provoking uncertainty and curiosity in reader/audience over who will remain 'dead'. This returns to the foreground the provisionality of theatrical death – the pleasure of fiction, entertainment and play, to be revived with every performance – and recalls Antonio's comical emergence from the coffin, very much alive, in *Antonio and Mellida*.[29]

The refusal to grant an 'end' or climax to pleasure – either tragic or comic – could further be explored with reference to the 'endings' of the respective plays. *Antonio and Mellida* seemed to follow the 'natural' course of a comedy: '[moving] from hostility and cruel jokes toward affection and shared humour',[30] with a 'new society crystallis[ing]' around the couple, conforming to Northrop Frye's description of what he perceives as a dominant trend in Renaissance comedy.[31] This comic 'end' is apparently destabilised in the following play, *Antonio's Revenge*. Yet, religious retreat, the outcome for the revengers (*AR*, V. 6. 34–5), is, as Ayres notes, lighter punishment than that usually meted out in Kydian revenge tragedy. Lewis points out that:

> we should be better able to appreciate any writer's use of humour if we are aware of the alternative responses that may be available [...]: cognitive and affective roads not taken every time humour occurs.[32]

The routes not manifestly taken in tragicomedy are nonetheless present in audience/reader expectations – expectations activated in tragicomedy. While revenge tragedy tends to culminate in escalating destruction and

---

29   Similarities throughout the plays suggest that *Hamlet* may be one of the plays parodied.

30   Lewis, *Comic Effects*, p. 45.

31   See Northrop Frye, *Anatomy of Criticism: Four Essays* (Princeton: Princeton University Press, 1957).

32   Lewis, *Comic Effects*, p. 26.

violence, though not lacking in comical excess or 'cruel laughter',[33] Marston attempts a more equal interplay of genres. Lewis' comment on the tragic vision as tending to overwhelm humorous diversions is relevant here: 'In the world of tragedy, [...] humour will do to lighten or darken the odd scene, but it cannot prevail.'[34] In Marston's *Antonio* plays on the other hand, Balurdo's participation in Piero's murder shows humour unvanquished.

The 'Tragic' in the 'Tragicomic'

We should recall here too Aristotle's belief that tragedy should constitute a more coherently unified 'whole' and 'end in misfortune',[35] which typically entails death and 'suffering' for the tragic hero – in Renaissance revenge plays, this falls upon the revenger, yet Antonio is spared this fate – thus the audience is also denied a tragic 'end'.[36]

Piero's glee is undercut by the fool Balurdo's entry, beard half-on half-off, as if interrupted in the process of getting dressed for the role ('I must be forced to conclude – the tiring man hath not glued on my beard half fast enough' (*AR*, II. 1. 30–1)). The mockery of Piero's pretentions to grandeur

33   Consider the empty box in *The Spanish Tragedy*, for example. Pedringano, a hired killer, is sentenced to hang. His silence on the identity of those who hired him is assured by the promise of pardon contained in a box, which the Page tasked with its delivery knows to be empty – a fact revealed to the audience (but not to the character Pedringano) before the execution. Pedringano is lulled into overconfidence by the Page who stands aside and bolsters his spirits by pointing at the box; hopes buoyant, the condemned man boasts and jokes as he goes to the gallows, and is summarily 'turned off' – death the dismal 'punch-line' – before he can fully comprehend the finality and hopelessness of his situation. It is a cruel moment of dark 'gallows humour', where laughter is invited, yet feels darkly inappropriate, despite Pedringano's acknowledged guilt (*The Spanish Tragedy*, Act III. V-VI).

34   Lewis, *Comic Effects*, pp. 67–8.

35   Aristotle, *On the Art of Poetry*, trans. by T. S. Dorsch, in *Classical Literary Criticism* (Middlesex: Penguin Books, 1965), pp. 29–75 (p. 43 and p. 48).

36   Clifford Leech notes that even where catharsis as 'purification' might not be an adequate description for the effect of tragedy, tragedy nonetheless differs from comedy in there being 'no future for the dead hero' (Leech, *Tragedy* (London: Routledge, 1969), p. 59).

may provide an indication that Piero must be excluded for order to be restored. Yet, comic pleasure does not spring solely from Balurdo's foppish foolery, but it is generated through the clash between 'Piero's passion and Balurdo's deflating nonsense'.[37] Comic pleasure is here *dependent* on the tragic dimension, with the latter's element of 'passion'.

Henri Bergson's contention that 'laughter is incompatible with emotion'[38] is useful here – it allows comic pleasure to be derived from 'cruel' laughter. However, it is insufficient to explain the laughter in tragicomedy. The distancing of character in the first play's metatheatrical Induction sets up another intervening layer to alienate the reader/viewer. Yet, this alienation does not preclude 'tragic' emotional engagement in every case (as in the poignantly painful moment when revenging hero Antonio brutally murders Piero's pleading young son, Julio, 'guilty' only by association with his father, in *Antonio's Revenge*, III. 3).[39] The dual courting of engagement and alienation coerce/coax the reader/viewer into an unstable position, troubling easy alignment – an instability which teasingly manipulates response, occasionally metatheatrically sharing this 'secret' with the reader/viewer.

---

37   Reginald A. Foakes, 'John Marston's Fantastical Plays: *Antonio and Mellida* and *Antonio's Revenge*', *Philological Quarterly*, vol. 41, n°1 (1962), pp. 229–39 (p. 234).

38   Bergson, 'Laughter', p. 250.

39   The structure of revenge narratives tends to rely on a response (revenge) which exceeds and overtakes the 'originary' crime it comes too late to amend and reconstruct, opening up the margins for tragicomedy's excesses. The voracious code of 'Vengeance' harps on 'More!' (*AR*, III. 3. 68), and by such 'more' exceeds remits of justifiability – becoming, in its excess of arbitrary violence, a grotesque parody of authorised punishment and of the prerogative of 'divine' Justice itself ('O bounteous heaven!/I do adore thy justice', III. 3. 6–7, 'even like insatiate hell', III. 3. 68). It thereby invites the audience/reader to form her/his own critical judgement. I have previously explored this aspect of the revenge narrative in my paper, 'The Promethean Infinite Spiral: Dislocating Agency of Revenge', written with Vered Weiss, and delivered at the ASCA International Workshop, 'Dislocating Agency – Moving Objects', University of Amsterdam, April 2013. Derek Dunne has argued that the plays' critique targets the failings of the juridical system as Marston observed them ('"Partialitie in a Judge, is a Turpitude": Partial Judges and Judicious Revengers in Early Modern English Drama', in *The Emergence of Impartiality: Towards a History of Objectivity*, ed. by Kathryn Murphy and Anita Traninger (Leiden: Brill, 2013), pp. 171–88).

Chance and Overturning Certainty

One effect of the comic in tragicomedy is the opening up of the field of play and possible options. 'Tragedy, not comedy, limits its field of operation [being] a more closely regulated form of response to the ambiguities and dilemmas of humanity.'[40] Comedy, on the other hand, would seem to expand the available range of means of engagement. Ambiguities in tragicomedy are however, not generated solely by comedy, but – as I have suggested – by the interplay between the two. The interworking of tragic and comic in the *Antonio* plays may be a joint pursuit, where solutions and problems counter each other as competing strands and account for the unapologetic magnitude of effect in both camps. Wiggins suggests that one source of the pleasure yielded by tragicomedy, and the 'central experience in which it trades, is audience relief at the transcendence of tragedy's limitations'.[41] Sypher notes that comedy 'can freely yield its action to surprise, chance'.[42] There is a suggestion of pleasurable surrendering to such 'chance' here, but also the opportunity for renewed means of engagement. Chance encounters, and sudden surprises, proliferate in both *Antonio* plays. The astonishing speed and frequency of 'chance' encounters in the two plays however inevitably suggest theatrical contrivance, undercutting randomness and chance. In G. K. Hunter's view, the characters become 'manipulable functions of [an] ironic structure', reminiscent of Aristotelian tragedy's subordination of character to plot.[43] As Hunter points out, the audience/reader enjoys greater awareness than is permitted the characters. We could extend this to dawning metatheatrical awareness of the plays' own manipulation of audience/reader. The *trompe l'oeil* between and within the two plays exposes audience/reader expectations precisely by *disappointing* them.[44] Our vision may indeed be

40   Sypher, *Comedy*, p. 206.
41   Wiggins, *Shakespeare and the Drama of His Time*, p. 119.
42   Sypher, *Comedy*, p. 219.
43   G. K. Hunter, in John Marston, *Antonio and Mellida: The First Part*, ed. by G. K. Hunter (London: Edward Arnold, 1965), pp. xiv–xv.
44   'Now there remains no discord that can sound/Harsh accents to the ear of our accord' (*Antonio and Mellida*, V. 2. 251–2). Slightly more ominous, in the suggestion that there is still room for derailment: 'O may the passage most successful

privileged by dramatic irony as far as characters are concerned, yet our awareness is only partial – due partly to the excessive leap ahead through expectations, which selectively pick out and re-order clues from the bewildering supply on offer. The plays' structure seems to calculatedly and actively play upon (and with) audience expectations, pre-empting, reshaping, challenging them – thus involving the very act of [mis]reading in the 'puzzle' of the plays. This unsettling of the basis of trust – related to the transformative ability of parody –[45] thrusts the reader/viewer into a complex relationship with the plays, which requires an active re-thinking of learned genre formulae while reading, and a renewed receptivity. The anticipatory excitement in uncertainty provokes a mixture of participation and submission to apparent 'chance'.

Oscillation and Incongruity

Characteristic of Marston's tragicomedy is this oscillation, which doesn't allow calm to settle – to modify Hamlet's final words, the rest can never be 'silence'; speech turns to babble, is interrupted. Antonio's tendency to exclaim in Latin has a fustian edge, and erupts both in heights of love, when 'standard' language will not suffice (*AM*, IV. 1. 189–227), and when solemnly, passionately yet ceremoniously, vowing revenge in terms of Senecan tragedy. This resolve, thus expressed, is interpreted by his mother as a sign of his 'mutining affections', prompting her to counsel him unceremoniously to 'go to bed' (*AR*, III. 2. 15–29). Tragic conventions are not permitted to run their course towards cathartic release – the pleasure traditionally associated with 'tragedy'; thus prompting a different view of pleasure.

   In Henri Bergson's terms, 'oscillation' from one feeling or state to another becomes something 'mechanical', yet comical because housed 'in something living'.[46] This may be borne out by the contrast between

---

prove' (*Antonio and Mellida*, V. 2. 264–5). Andrugio as Epilogue, promises: 'What imperfections you have seen in us, leave with us and we'll amend it' (*Antonio and Mellida*, Epilogue 4–5).

45   See Genette, *Palimpsests*, p. 5.

46   Bergson, 'Laughter', p. 110.

theatrical device (highlighted almost excessively in tragicomedy)[47] and the living actors that inhabit (embodying) the roles – a discrepancy made physical onstage, but also signposted in the play-text. The oscillations in Marston's *Antonio* plays seem to go from extreme to extreme. Brooke notes that each genre in its extremity is liable to turn to laughter.[48] Though comic and tragic heroes 'alike "learn through suffering"', Sypher notes that typically 'suffering in comedy takes the form of humiliation, disappointment, or chagrin, instead of death.'[49] This distinction does not hold true for the *Antonio* plays, where both outcomes occur in tandem, yet 'learning' is limited (leading to repetition, rather than satisfactory resolution). This vacillation between extremes challenges expectations for either genre, and prompts Ann Blake to conclude 'the style is thus the outcome of Marston's practice of driving his characters to the brink of what they can endure, […] and then recording their reactions'.[50] The nearness of risk and thinness of the veil separating extremes may provide a thrill all its own in *Antonio and Mellida*, for – to quote Henri Bergson –[51] when 'every moment the whole thing threatens to break down, but manages to get patched up again; it is this diversion that excites laughter', as 'the reciprocal interference of series' coincide where they are assumed to be distinct.

Comic repetition and detachment serve furthermore to defer tragedy's desired climax. The arbitrariness of character in performance is revealed by the theatricality of costume-changes, role-doubling (e.g. Alberto doubles as Andrugio, *AM*, Induction 21–3), the instability of disguise and series of failed recognitions. The operation of *katharsis*, whence springs the pleasure particular to 'tragedy' in Aristotle's conception, is predicated upon fear

---

47   Reginald A. Foakes, 'Tragicomedy and Comic Form', in *Comedy from Shakespeare to Sheridan: Change and Continuity in the English and European Dramatic Tradition*, ed. by A. R. Braunmuller and J. C. Bulman (Newark: University of Delaware Press, 1986), pp. 74–88 (p. 82).

48   Brooke, *Horrid Laughter in Jacobean Tragedy*, p. 3.

49   Sypher, *Comedy*, p. 254.

50   Ann Blake, '"The Humour of Children": John Marston's Plays in the Private Theatres', *Review of English Studies*, New Series, vol. 38, n°152 (1987), pp. 471–82 (p. 479).

51   Bergson, 'Laughter', p. 124.

and pity, which require a degree of empathy as well as distance.[52] Antonio's chameleonic disguises (including an Amazon, a sailor and a Fool) trouble empathetic identification, by failing to provide a consistent and centred point of reference.

Foolery and Play

The manifestations of 'foolery' in the plays constitute another important source of tragicomic pleasure. Here again, the comic interacts with the tragic, and turns emotional intensity to pleasure in play. The actor's potential to be many parts in one is matched by the character's shape-shifting capacity. An Induction that brings the actors forth actively highlights the oddness of 'two' occupying the same space *and* time. The awareness this evokes undercuts representational convention. Weimann suggests the legacy of the fool show and oral culture might persist in such situations, where the performer was 'not altogether "lost" in what he performed', with more unfettered 'playfulness' taking its place beside purpose.[53]

Metatheatricality here has a particular affinity with comic pleasure and play. Drawing upon the same tradition as Weimann, Willeford describes the Fool's disguise as one 'which partly creates an illusion and partly violates it'.[54] The series of disguises and the highlighting of character-as-role suggest that duality, split and play of partial substitutions constitute a 'central' concern of the plays, and determine relations between characters as well as their function. Thus, a contrast such as that between Balurdo and Piero implies more than a collision between worlds – the 'worlds' are not separate, but rather they affect each other. Even 'locus' characters, such as Piero, maintain openness in their incompleteness, and in such cases, it seems the comic has the upper hand: 'It is a major activity of the Fool

52   See Aristotle, *On the Art of Poetry*, p. 39.

53   Robert Weimann, 'Performance-Game and Representation in *Richard III*', in *Textual and Theatrical Shakespeare: Questions of Evidence*, ed. by Edward Pechter (Iowa City: University of Iowa Press, 1996), pp. 66–85 (p. 68).

54   William Willeford, *The Fool and His Sceptre: A Study in Clowns and Jesters and Their Audience* (Chicago: Northwestern University Press, 1969), p. 54.

to make a fool of other people.'[55] Fools are multiplied, foolery shared, as Antonio disguises himself as professional Fool at Piero's court (*AR*, IV. 2). With the impertinence and equivocation due to a fool, Antonio exposes similarities, as well as differences between himself-as-fool and Piero, and furthermore manoeuvres the Fool into a more central plot-related position, while retaining the right to comment on the action.

Balurdo, the habitual fool, seems to bear 'the fool's immortality' (a feature Antonio seems to share, in his parries with, and cheatings of, death), a characteristic which Willeford suggests causes 'conflict [to be] reduced to play'.[56] Bakhtin's notion of the 'double-voicedness' of parody involves re-accentuation with repetition.[57] Balurdo's decontextualising repetition of newly learned words such as 'obtuse' and 'retort' in the most inappropriate of contexts empties them of 'meaning', revealing affectation in others' speech, and by extension, recalls the nature of performance. The notion that language is detachable from character and source destabilises another point of possible connection with the characters-as-characters. The suggested hollowness of words is the source of their power to generate disturbing and/or comically parodic echoes. Gair observes that Marston sought linguistic innovation, using 'as many newly coined words and phrases (originating a very large proportion of these himself) as possible'.[58] This linguistic innovativeness takes up abode within the 'standard' – the attempted disarticulation to ' "uh" or nothing' (*AM*, V. 1. 30), if ultimately impossible ('It cannot be done, sir, but by a seeming kind of drunkenness', *AM*, V. 1. 31), serves the purpose of defamiliarising the already-known. This relates to the parodic interplay between different tones and genres, a parodic thrust

---

55   William Empson, *The Structure of Complex Words* (New York: New Directions, 1951), pp. 107–8.

56   Willeford, *The Fool and His Sceptre*, p. 137. Contrast this with a later instance of a Fool's mortality: where the Fool is mortal and the death shown on stage, this tends to signal a shift in tone, and intensify the sense of an irreversible escalation towards the 'tragic' – such as Bergetto's violent death onstage (the result indeed of comic devices of mistaken identity, chance and accident – here more cruel in their consequence) in John Ford's *'Tis Pity She's a Whore*.

57   Bakhtin, *Problems of Dostoevsky's Poetics*, pp. 194–5.

58   Reavley Gair, in Marston, *Antonio's Revenge*, p. 21.

which cannot be dissociated from a 'comic effect' in language, highlighting a discrepancy or disproportion which triggers appreciative surprise and recognition of the always-present possibility of ambiguities.

As previously mentioned, the Induction immediately draws attention to the boy-actors (the Children of Paul's). The acknowledgement of limitations and inadequacy is a step towards opening up the space for the 'comic', and for self-conscious 'play'. Parody draws force from discrepancies and contradictions which resist resolution, and from a refusal to smooth over the seams rendered visible in inadequate superimposition of character-over-actor. Indeed, one view of parody would oppose it to pastiche on the grounds of transformations involved – in contrast to travesty, which would modify style but not rank, parody in this view plays on a disjunction between subject and a retained 'elevated' style.[59] This kind of parody enters here on the metatheatrical level, touching upon the very construction of characters and layering of structure. It draws the audience/reader's attention to the incongruity of ill-fitting roles which require child-actors to 'frame exterior shape/To haughty form of elate majesty' (*AM*, Induction, 7–12). The size/age discrepancy specific to the boy companies accentuates a trait that applies across the acting profession more generally. Actors may play kings, courtiers and other roles betokening power – a temporary 'usurpation' that might enable, alongside the potential for parody, a critique of such power (as in Shakespeare's *Henry V*).[60] The heightened alertness the *Antonio* plays demand of the reader/viewer, refusing safe refuge in established convention and withdrawing certainties, encourages a critical stance through parody – suggesting another source of pleasure.

We should note here that the actors' 'detachment from their roles' that Foakes stresses is meticulously scripted.[61] The Page's comment on the 'confusion of Babel' that is the lovers' scripted-unscripted exchange in Latin is symptomatic of the paradox: the Page apologises for this sudden

59   Genette, *Palimpsests*, p. 22.

60   Jonathan Dollimore and Alan Sinfield argue, I think rightly, that *Henry V* resists reading in terms of a unified dominant ideology ('History and Ideology: The Instance of *Henry V*', in *Alternative Shakespeares*, ed. by John Drakakis (London: Methuen, 1985), pp. 206–27 (p. 211)).

61   Foakes, 'John Marston's Fantastical Plays', p. 230.

change in language, stating, ''tis an error easier to be pardoned by the auditors' than excused by the author's' (*AM*, IV. 1. 219–26); this suggests an *appearance* of spontaneous improvisation. These scripted 'deviations' from the script are not straining merely against the bounds of the page, but like Marston's play with language, are symptomatic of a striving against limitations in more general terms[62] – those of performance-space as well as page: 'O, for time and place long enough and large enough to act these fools! Here might be made a rare scene of folly, if the plot could bear it'. (*AM*, III. 2. 117–19) Even fools therefore prove subject to the constraints of the 'frame' – comedy may widen the range of responses, but – as with the tragic dimension – it too cannot provide full release from the enthralling tension within/between the plays, returning us to the interplay at the fissured heart of Marston's tragicomedy.

While Antonio ultimately bears the 'immortality' usually associated with the Fool figure (a figure he only assumes, as one in a series of disguises), this is a security which is not obviously guaranteed. The disguise itself is more temporary and contingent than the character's underlying identity as 'Antonio', and doubly underlined as a performance-within-a-performance. The role of 'revenger' on the other hand is seemingly demanded by the plot. Yet in a counterintuitive reversal this is revealed to be ultimately less crucial in determining the fate of Antonio (which would typically be death, in a revenge tragedy), than a Fool's disguise. The latter disguise is moreover explicitly highlighted as unnecessary play and frivolity through the protests of other characters. Alberto, a fellow 'Gentleman of the Court', lists a number of alternative disguises that he deems preferable and more effective: 'Rather put on some trans-shaped cavalier,/Some habit of a spitting critic, [...] rather assume –'. Antonio cuts him short, reaffirming the value of performance, for this – he points out – is a role which enables something approaching a greater purity of 'affectation', a superfluous disguise which doesn't involve inhabiting the 'very flesh', but which can be put on and discarded

---

62   Hunter sees this passage as Marston's attempt to find a 'love-strain more remote from everyday conversation than anything he could achieve in English' (Marston, *Antonio and Mellida*, p. xx).

(*Antonio's Revenge*, IV. 1. 2–9). The Fool's freedom is enabled by the very act of performance and of play, a realm which hinges on the celebration of arbitrariness and inconsistency – the pleasure of the game, even in defiance of genre-driven plot. Antonio's borrowing of the 'Fool's habit', while straddling a position which allows him to have an impact on the plot, opens up the possibility of divergent routes.

Conclusion

The inconsistencies and oscillations within the plays have provoked as many differences in interpretation. Blake reads 'a psychological pattern' into 'these transformations if man is seen as the slave of passion',[63] while Samuel Schoenbaum names Marston as the slave of his own raging passions, incapable of doing more than letting his 'disordered fancies' tumble out in some confusion.[64] Jensen suggests almost complete disconnection between the Induction and the plays, asserting that 'there is almost no evidence to persuade the reader that the tone of the "Induction" is the dominant tone of the play it introduces'.[65] I would suggest, on the contrary, that the uncertainties of tone noted here would seem to be the most paradoxically consistent feature in the *Antonio* plays – where the balance between comic and tragic is unstable, unpredictable and shifting, with the two frequently sharing the stage (as in Piero's murder). The pleasure is to be found not in attempting to piece it all into one cohesive mass, but in destabilisation itself – the acceptance of the hybridity of the whole, and interaction with the disjunctions that riddle it.

---

63   Blake, 'The Humour of Children', p. 479.
64   Samuel Schoenbaum, 'The Precarious Balance of John Marston', *PMLA*, vol. 67, n°7 (1952), pp. 1069–78 (p. 1077).
65   Ejner J. Jensen, 'The Style of the Boy Actors', *Comparative Drama*, vol. 2, n°2 (1968), pp. 100–14 (p. 104).

Seen in relation to what Foakes identifies as the plays' hypotexts[66] ('earlier revenge plays'),[67] amongst which both Foakes and Ayres stress *The Spanish Tragedy*, the expectations for the ending would be unfulfilled, teasingly invoked only to be disappointed, another withheld punch-line. The contrast this time is not between the two plays, but is a contrast set up in relation to viewers' expectations, enabling parody by disproving and destabilising the 'possible world' interwoven of the intertextual 'encyclo-paedias' that constitute their store of knowledge,[68] and evoked by the play. The kind of 'trickery' in Marston's tragicomedy has more in line with the comic process that:

> turn[s] on itself […] to produce pleasure from the exposure of its own shortcomings, 'embracing the instabilities of discourse'. One function of the unworked text, then, is to play the role of trickster […] exposing the trickery which sustains the myth of the finished literary masterwork, and reactivating the literary game in the bizarre hope of not winning.[69]

The problematic (and conventionally unsatisfying) ending, the interminable reversals, repetitions and reactivations are all part of Marston's 'game' in these plays. Yet, if the punch-line is withheld, so is catharsis – the pleasure to be derived therefore is not one of release, either from the comic game or from the tragic scene – instead, 'suf-fering' is here closely linked to 'teasing', the violence is linked to play. The violence itself *plays*, and the 'extremes' – rather than promising and delivering climax – are caught up in the oscillating movement of tone, plot, character and action.

66   I here use Genette's term for the parodied text: 'By hypertextuality I mean any re-lationship uniting a text B (which I shall call the hypertext) to an earlier text A (I shall, of course, call it the hypotext) upon which it is grafted in a manner that is not that of commentary' (Genette, *Palimpsests*, p. 5), although it may have this add-itional function (*ibid.*, p. 8).

67   Foakes, 'John Marston's Fantastical Plays', pp. 232–3.

68   Umberto Eco, *The Role of the Reader: Explorations in the Semiotics of Texts* (Bloomington: Indiana University Press, 1984), p. 217 and p. 208.

69   Jerry Aline Flieger, *The Purloined Punch Line: Freud's Comic Theory and the Postmodern Text* (Baltimore: The John Hopkins University Press, 1991), p. 52. Flieger here explores comedy in terms of Blanchot's 'unworking' of text.

Parody lays bare aspects of its target-texts and genres and reveals something about the quality of the pleasure derived. Just as parody could only work in relation to its parodied genre/text,[70] depending on it for comic effect, so tragicomedy requires the interrelationship (and tension) between tragedy and comedy to be sustained. Although my argument has tended to foreground the play of the comic, it is housed within a tragicomic world which permits more violent excesses. This tragicomic world courts the possibility of more violent repercussions, including death – a possibility sometimes final, sometimes suspended, sometimes seemingly forgotten or diverted, sometimes held in sight (even physically – through the presence of coffins and ghosts), and sometimes shown to be a threat defused (as in the provisionality of stage-death) – challenging predictability and certainty. The pleasure is, therefore, also linked to uncertainty, the multiplying of possibilities troubling a recognisable framework from within, triggering a kind of ongoing 'guessing game'.

The interplay between the genres in these plays produces an instability and uncertainty that, therefore, resists being subsumed within either genre, and as we have seen, the two are in such close proximity and the oscillations so sudden, that they seem often to occupy the same space. Moreover, the comic dimension in the plays proves to be more than occasional relief, or even than a constant fantastically shaped parodic shadow, tagged along – Balurdo's intrusions burst in at the potentially most tragically loaded moments, and like Andrugio's ghost, the parodic double refuses to hover in liminality. The audience's and reader's pleasure is, then, inseparable from a degree of apprehension. Such 'tragicomic' pleasure is derived from oscillations, incongruities, instabilities, the interaction between the comic and the tragic and the teasing-tickling deferral of climax and catharsis. In Marston's *Antonio* plays, such pleasure-without-final-satisfaction plays with the reader's expectations and response. Pleasure partly arises from comedy's 'threat' to excessive seriousness, and from the (scripted) seemingly aleatory interplay. Comedy's restoration of order itself proves susceptible to overturning, as in the first play's 'deceptive' ending, and the second play's withholding of full cathartic release.

---

70   Hutcheon, *A Theory of Parody*, p. 26.

PART III

Barthes and Japan, the 'Empire of Signs'

Signifiance and Undialectical Writing

FABIEN ARRIBERT-NARCE

6 Taking Signs for What They Are

Roland Barthes, Chris Marker and the Pleasure of *Texte Japon*

Roland Barthes and Chris Marker discovered Japan roughly at the same time, in the mid-1960s, when the country was fast developing and started to impress the rest of the world for its architectural and technological feats – widely displayed during the 1964 Tokyo Olympics. Incidentally, their respective works dedicated to this object of fascination *par excellence* tend to share a similar approach to Japanese culture, that they both represent from a very personal perspective. In Barthes's *Empire of Signs* (*L'Empire des signes*, 1970), a broad-ranging photo-text meditating in particular on society, art and literature and Marker's *Sunless* (*Sans soleil*, 1982), an experimental, unclassifiable documentary film combining images of Iceland, Guinea-Bissau and Japan to reflect on the nature of memory, the two French authors purposely select and emphasise the 'features' of Japanese everyday life, art and culture that captivated them the most, while clearly acknowledging that as 'outsiders' not understanding Japanese language they are bound to produce an external and inaccurate representation of this country; their perception of it cannot escape the Western categories which constitute their intellectual and sensual selves. In other words, Japanese people might not recognise 'their' Japan, their values and societal background in *Empire of Signs* and *Sunless*. This does not mean however that these two works do not have important things to tell us about several aspects of this culture and its specificity. According to Maurice Pinguet, the former Director of the Franco-Japanese Institute in Tokyo (1963–8) who first invited Barthes to Japan and introduced him to its artistic and social traditions, what makes such works particularly interesting is precisely that they 'offer a multi-faceted presentation of their object, thanks to a sharp sense of observation and from angles that are usually neglected by specialists';[1] it is from this perspective that Pinguet analysed in his essay entitled 'Le texte Japon'[2] Barthes's exploration of the pleasure of 'Japan-as-text' in *Empire of Signs*.

A similar idea was more recently expressed by Philippe Forest, another contemporary French writer fascinated by Japan:

> Writing, reading [about Japanese culture], I might have been mistaken. I am certainly still mistaken. But I have always been convinced that my mistakes opened for me a singular and necessary path towards truth. Who could judge somebody else's dream?[3]

In *La Beauté du contresens* (2005), this was theorised by Forest as 'beautiful misinterpretations' in the context of transcultural relations, in reference to a remark made by Marcel Proust in *Contre Sainte-Beuve*:[4] 'Beautiful books are written in a sort of foreign language. Beneath each word each one of us puts his own meaning or at least his own image, which is often a misinterpretation. But in beautiful books all our misinterpretations are beautiful.' This approach shouldn't be understood as an excuse used by those who do not make the effort to learn a foreign language and to assimilate another cultural background, but rather as an invitation to take the works analysed in this chapter for what they are, that is, creative travelogues more or less accurately informed, and offering a subjective and intuitive gaze on a perceived reality. If numerous critics often referring to post-colonial theory have rightly pinpointed the orientalist and exoticist stereotypes, essentialisations and misunderstandings in Barthes's essay and – to a lesser extent – Marker's film (e.g. about Zen

1   Maurice Pinguet, *Le Texte Japon, introuvables et inédits*, ed. by Michaël Ferrier (Paris: Seuil, 2009), p. 31; my translation.

2   Pinguet, 'Le texte Japon' (1982), in *Le Texte Japon*, pp. 29–43.

3   Philippe Forest, *Haiku, etc. Allaphbed 4* (Nantes: Cécile Defaut, 2008), p. 15; my translation.

4   See Philippe Forest, *La Beauté du contresens et autres essais sur la littérature japonaise* (Nantes: Cécile Défaut, 2005), pp. 11–29.

Buddhism or haiku poems),[5] one should also keep in mind that one of the central elements of their respective reflections in and on Japan concerns signs, their production and reception, within and outside the realm of meaning and significations; encountering a civilisation whose customs and language they didn't know well, both authors didn't claim to produce specialist discourse and were instead inclined to question the very readability of signs. In this respect, their works address issues related in particular to the difference between 'seeing' and 'reading', that is, intermedial breaches and stitches, that their singular responses to Japanese signs and their alleged specificities bring to light and interrogate.

Being at the same time one of the world's laboratories for the production of new signs and icons since the end of the Second World War and a universe in which systems of signification and codes are extremely developed and sophisticated, Japan offered to Barthes and Marker a unique opportunity to reflect on the reception of emotional and cognitive stimulations and of material signs and signals. In this context, they were naturally led to detach significations from signifiers, whose visual dimension particularly fascinated them in this country. As we shall see, their works eventually question how we respond to texts and images in general, which raises the issue of the pleasure experienced by the reader/viewer; they also promote another way to apprehend the countless cultural signs that surround us, in Japan and beyond.

Roland Barthes and the Empire of *Signifiance*

Barthes made three stays in Japan between 1966 and 1967. From this experience, he wrote *Empire of Signs* which marked a personal turn in his writing. After the publication of this essay in 1970, his texts are indeed

5   See for instance the critical essays listed by Charles Forsdick in his article ' "(In) connaissance de l'Asie": Barthes and Bouvier, China and Japan', which analyse *L'Empire des signes* in the light of a post-colonial critique of Orientalism (in *Modern & Contemporary France*, vol. 14, n°1 (2006), pp. 63–77 (p. 69)).

less concerned by the adoption of a rigorous scientific method and tend
to use a more personal tone. In this book that opened what is often referred to as his 'post-structuralist' period, and which can be described as
a travelogue mainly focusing – like his *Mythologies* (1957) – on various
aspects of everyday life (food, houses, gestures, stores, train stations …),
he nonetheless addresses an essential question, that of the production of
meaning. How does a sign *signify*, and communicate to us its meaning or
message? His answer to this question has remained the same since his first
essays published in the 1950s: signs are cultural products, their meaning is
arbitrary and depends on the context of their production and reception.
In other words, the meaning of a sign is not natural, and can change and
evolve over time. But in *Empire of Signs*, Barthes goes one step further
and expresses for the first time his desire to escape what he calls 'Western
semiocracy', that is, the tyranny of meaning and dominance of the 'full'
sign;[6] he more specifically criticises the Western obsession to give or find
meaning in everything, and the process of *making sense* – to use his own
words, 'the West moistens everything with meaning'.[7] In his view, Japan
provides an ideal framework to develop this critic given its idiosyncratic
approach to signs and to meaning: 'in this country (Japan) the empire of
signifiers is so immense, so in excess of speech, that the exchange of signs
remains of a fascinating richness, mobility, and subtlety, despite the opacity of the language, sometimes even as a consequence of that opacity.'[8]

Barthes's creative method and ethos in *Empire of Signs* is quite simple: it
consists in (re)writing what he calls '*his* Japan'.[9] This is why he claims in
the opening section of the book that 'the author has never, in any sense,
photographed Japan'.[10] By this Barthes means that his essay is in no way
a tourist guidebook aiming to (re)present the 'real' Japan as accurately as

6   Barthes, *Empire of Signs*, back cover.
7   *Ibid.*, p. 70.
8   *Ibid.*, pp. 9–10.
9   As Maurice Pinguet puts it, 'Japan, that Japan, his Japan – was the utopia of desir-
     able for Roland Barthes' (*Le Texte Japon*, p. 20; my translation).
10   Barthes, *Empire of Signs*, p. 4. In the same section of the text, Barthes also
     writes in relation to Japan: 'I, in no way, claim to represent or to analyse reality
     itself' (*ibid.*, p. 3).

possible – which does not mean of course it is not anchored in the reality of Japan, in its everyday life as the French semiologist was able to experience it during his few visits to the country. The key point Barthes is trying to convey is that his book is that of a writer, an artist and not a collection of postcard-like clichés. It is in this sense that the following statement from *The Preparation of the Novel*, his Lecture Courses at the Collège de France in 1978–9 and 1979–80, should be understood, in relation to the method of writing he used in *Empire of Signs* and other books: ' "My" doesn't refer, or doesn't *ultimately* refer, to an egotism, a narcissism […] but to a Method: method of exposition, method of speech.'[11]

Writing on '*his*' Japan', Barthes focused on a number of features of Japanese culture that particularly fascinated him, approaching them not only with his intellect, but also and perhaps primarily with his body – 'corps' is a recurring word in *Empire of Signs*, used dozens of times.[12] He thus turned his singular situation – not being familiar with Japanese language and cultural codes – into an opportunity, which allowed him to concentrate on the materiality of signs. This is epitomised by the following remark made in the second section of the book, 'The Unknown Language':

> The dream: to know a foreign (alien) language and yet not to understand it: to perceive the difference in it without that difference ever being recuperated by the superficial sociality of discourse […]; in a word, to descend into the untranslatable, to experience its shock without ever muffling it, until everything Occidental in us totters and the rights of the 'father tongue' vacillate […]. The murmuring mass of an unknown language constitutes a delicious protection, envelops the foreigner (provided the country is not hostile to him) in an auditory film which halts at his ears all the alienations of the mother tongue.[13]

11 Roland Barthes, *The Preparation of the Novel: Lecture Courses and Seminars at the Collège de France, 1978–1979 and 1979–1980*, trans. by Kate Briggs (New York: Columbia University Press, 2010), p. 23. In these lectures, which were completed just weeks before his death in 1980, Barthes evokes for the first time his desire to write a novel.

12 In *The Pleasure of the Text* (New York: Hill and Wang, 1975), Barthes goes as far as claiming that 'The pleasure of the text is that moment when my body pursues its own ideas – for my body does not have the same ideas I do' (p. 17).

13 Barthes, *Empire of Signs*, pp. 6–9. As Charles Forsdick rightly noted, 'Language (or the traveller's ignorance of it) plays a key role in *L'Empire des signes*, with

As indicated by the title of his essay, Barthes perceived Japan as an 'empire of signs', that is, a very complex assemblage of images and texts that he could 'read', but only if 'reading' is understood here as a kind of writing – or even rewriting. To illustrate this with a telling example, let us consider what he writes about the Japanese art of flower arrangement (*ikebana*) in the section of the book entitled 'Packages':

> the Japanese bouquet has a volume; unknown masterpiece […], you can move your body into the interstice of its branches, into the space of its stature, not in order to *read* it (to read its symbolism) but to follow the trajectory of the hand which has written it: a true writing, since it produces a volume and since, forbidding our reading to be the simple decoding of a message […], it permits this reading to repeat the course of the writing's labour.[14]

The Japanese bouquet is presented here like a sign, a kind of written text. Barthes does not attempt to grasp its potential meaning, its symbolism; instead, he reads and 'rewrites' it at the same time, 'repeating the course of the writing's labour' as he puts it. In other words, he invests it physically, sensuously. This is, according to him, a Westerner, one of the specificities of Japanese signs: their reading does not imply the decoding of a message, but a process of (re)writing, of physical investment. In this respect, his detour via Japan allowed Barthes to express this essential motto that defined the later phase of his career, and in the light of which one can better understand some of the comments in *Empire of Signs* which seem to contradict the author's earlier work on semiology; for instance, although it has often been argued that one of the key messages of this book is that 'Meaning is secondary. It is halted by the emptiness of signs, their inability to stand outside of a conventional – and therefore arbitrary – system of representation that has produced them according to its own cultural logic',[15] what matters most for Barthes is rather the erotics of writerly[16]

---

untranslatability, both practical and metaphorical, transformed into a source of pleasure' (Forsdick, '(In)connaissance de l'Asie', pp. 72–3).

14   Barthes, *Empire of Signs*, p. 45.

15   Peter Pericles Trifonas, *Barthes and the Empire of Signs* (Cambridge: Icon Books, 2001), p. 15.

16   In *S/Z*, Barthes suggests that the goal of a 'writerly' (or '*scriptible*') text is 'to make the reader no longer a consumer but a producer of the text' (*S/Z*, trans. by Richard

signs he is aiming to develop through his encounter with Japan – literally his *pre-text* in this situation.

As we have seen, a section of *Empire of Signs* focuses on Japanese packages, which are representative of all the signs encountered in this culture according to Barthes. Referring in particular to decorative sake barrels, he suggests in this respect that:

> one can already see a true semantic meditation in the merest Japanese package. [...] The box acts the sign: as envelope, screen, mask, it is worth what it conceals, protects, and yet designates. [...] from envelope to envelope, the signified flees, and when you finally have it (there is always a little *something* in the package), it appears insignificant, laughable, vile: the pleasure, field of the signifier, has been taken: the package is not empty, but emptied.[17]

This suggests that the reception of Japanese signs differs in Barthes's mind from the traditional structure of the sign, combining a signifier and a signified to produce a message – and meaning. The package is more important than its content – what it conceals, and if we follow Barthes's logic, Japanese signifiers are, generally speaking, at least as important as their signifieds (their literal signification), which are described as 'insignificant, laughable, vile'. Although the overgeneralisation and simplification on which this claim relies is problematic, the short apologue in which it is presented by Barthes allows him to draw here some key, wide-ranging lessons about the pleasure of the text; these can be related once more to the emblematic example of foreign languages (*for him*): 'The unknown language, of which I nonetheless grasp the respiration, the emotive aeration, in a word the pure significance, forms around me, as I move, a faint vertigo, sweeping me into its artificial emptiness, which is consummated only for me: I live in the interstice, delivered from any fulfilled meaning.'[18]

This implies that when Barthes uses the paradoxical and often misleading expression 'empty signs' in his essay, he actually refers to signs

---

Miller (New York: Hill and Wang, 1974, p. 4)). In this perspective, reading becomes 'not a parasitical act, the reactive complement of a writing', but rather a 'form of work' (*ibid.*, p. 10).

17   Barthes, *Empire of Signs*, pp. 45–6.
18   *Ibid.*, p. 9.

whose significations have naturally not disappeared, but rather been suspended – a process he calls 'exemption from meaning' in the title of a
section dedicated to haiku writing and Zen Buddhism. In this context,
Japanese signs are not empty but *emptied* (for Barthes); they can be defined as signifiers whose signifieds have been dismissed because they are
not fully accessible to the Western reader/viewer.[19] But these signifiers
never cease to express something, despite the neutralisation of the search
for meaning – which can be obsessional and distracting; they remain pleasurable and appealing: Barthes evokes 'a shock of meaning lacerated, ex-
tenuated to the point of its irreplaceable void, without the object's ever
ceasing to be significant, desirable';[20] 'the pleasure, field of the signifier, has
been taken: the package is not empty, but emptied.'[21] 'Empire of signifiers'
rather than 'signs' would therefore be a more accurate and less ambiguous
title for this work. Barthes's 'Japan-as-text' is not really, or not primarily,
'a text whose surface phenomena operate as signs to be deciphered',[22] but
rather savoured and enjoyed; in this empire, everything is considered as
writing (faces, gardens, flower arrangements, bunraku puppets, violence,
etc.) that should be appreciated for its material qualities, its 'layering of significance' –[23] that is, 'meaning, *insofar* as it is *sensually produced*' to borrow
the definition of *signifiance* in *The Pleasure of the Text*.[24] We remember
here that reading such signs implies rewriting them for Barthes, following
the model of calligraphy that fascinated him because of its proximity with
painting. As he asks in *Empire of Signs* in relation to a calligraphed haiku
accompanied by a drawing: 'Where does the writing begin? Where does

19   Kōjin Karatani has rightly defined this exemption or 'bracketing' process as an ex-
     ample of 'aestheticentricm', particularly well-spread among post-war French intel-
     lectuals and artists. He criticised this attitude for its orientalist and exoticist over-
     tones. See Karatani's article 'Uses of Aesthetics: After Orientalism', *Boundary Two*,
     vol. 25, n°2 (1998), pp. 145–60.
20   Barthes, *Empire of Signs*, p. 4.
21   *Ibid.*, p. 46.
22   Forsdick, '(In)connaissance de l'Asie', p. 70.
23   Barthes, *The Pleasure of the Text*, p. 12.
24   *Ibid.*, p. 61. Elsewhere in the text, Barthes also notes: 'The text is language without
     its image-reservoir […] significance, bliss – that is precisely what withdraws the
     text from the image-systems of language' (*ibid.*, p. 33).

the painting begin?'[25] Barthes distances himself from a utilitarian or scientific approach to signs and suggests that signifiers, be they verbal, visual or of a different type, should be first and foremost tasted and enjoyed for what they are (i.e. the *significance* of the signifier to use his terms), which is an end in itself to his mind: 'Text and image, interlacing, seek to ensure the circulation and exchange of these signifiers: body, face, writing; and in them to read the retreat of signs', that is to say the retreat of signification, of meaning.[26] As his friend and mentor Maurice Pinguet pointed out, 'this tendency to ignore the central function of the signifier can be found throughout the Western history, in the form of a denial'.[27]

All the signs that Barthes mentions in his essay could be described as 'fleshy' signs: food, packages, paintings, calligraphies, photographs, maps … He considers them as textual bodies defined by their colours, textures, tastes, sounds and the words that he uses most frequently to characterise them are volume, substance, surface, space and density. This forms the basis of his erotics of signs referred to earlier, this dimension being already pointed at by the very title of the book; the term 'empire' does not only designate Japan and its political regime, or by extension a space of utopia, 'faraway', but also alludes to the territory of the senses, to 'empirism' and carnal attraction, desire – the empiric power of signs. Once more, this helps us understand why Barthes reinstates the importance of the body (including his own) for his new ethics and aesthetics of signs theorised at the occasion of his encounter with Japan, and in response to its art and culture:

> in Japan the body exists, acts, shows itself, gives itself, without hysteria, without narcissism, but according to a pure – though subtly discontinuous – erotic project. […]. To make a date (by gestures, drawings on paper, proper names) may take an hour, but during that hour, for a message which would be abolished in an instant if it were to be spoken (simultaneously quite essential and quite insignificant), it is the other's entire body which has been known, savoured, received, and which has displayed (to no real purpose) its own narrative, its own text.[28]

25   Barthes, *Empire of Signs*, p. 21.
26   *Ibid.*, p. xi.
27   Pinguet, *Le Texte Japon*, p. 33; my translation.
28   Barthes, *Empire of Signs*, pp. 9–10.

It is also in this perspective that the French semiologist compared his encounter with Japan with 'certain modern texts' (e.g. by Philippe Sollers,
quoted in *Empire of Signs*), which 'open up the whole fictive realm' and
'permit us to perceive a landscape which our speech (the speech we own)
could under no circumstances either discover or divine' as he puts it.[29] In
these 'texts of bliss', as Barthes calls them in *The Pleasure of the Text*, like
in Japan-as-text, signifiers are detached from their signifieds;[30] meaning is
not immediately accessible to the reader, and not the primary purpose –
the text is conceived as a discontinuous, fragmented and flexible chain of
signifiers, and 'the very arcanum of signification, that is, the paradigm,
is rendered impossible'.[31] As we can see here, the 'empire of signs' understood as the power of the pleasure of the text has an emancipatory function, a liberating effect for the reader, dissolving the myth of the unity of
the self and the moral grip of ideology and prescriptive institutions:

> Imagine someone [...] who abolishes within himself all barriers, all classes, all ex-
> clusions, not by syncretism but by simple discard of that old spectre: logical contra-
> diction; who mixes every language, even those said to be incompatible; who silently
> accepts every charge of illogicality, of incongruity; [...] this anti-hero exists: he is
> the reader of the text at the moment he takes his pleasure. Thus the Biblical myth
> is reversed, the confusion of tongues is no longer a punishment, the subject gains
> access to bliss by the cohabitation of languages *working side by side*.[32]

One of the constant features of Japanese signs described by Barthes is that
they are always exposed as such, presenting themselves plainly as signs,
without initiating a paradigm between surface and depth, obvious and
hidden significations. Bunraku puppet theatre, in which puppeteers can

29 *Ibid.*, pp. 6–7.
30 Here is how Barthes defines texts of pleasure and of bliss in *The Pleasure of the Text*
    (p. 14): 'Text of pleasure: the text that contents, fills, grants euphoria; the text that
    comes from culture and does not break with it, is linked to a comfortable practice
    of reading. Text of bliss: the text that imposes a state of loss, the text that discom-
    forts (perhaps to the point of a certain boredom), unsettles the reader's historical,
    cultural, psychological assumptions, the consistency of his tastes, values, memories,
    brings to a crisis his relation with language.'
31 Barthes, *Empire of Signs*, p. 73.
32 Barthes, *The Pleasure of the Text*, pp. 3–4.

be seen by the audience, is a good example of this. But this characteristic is also emblematically shared by haiku poems as they are defined by Barthes:

> the haiku has the purity, the sphericality, and the very emptiness of a note of music; perhaps that is why it is spoken twice, in echo; [...] to speak it many times would postulate that meaning is to be discovered in it, would simulate profundity; between the two, neither singular nor profound, the echo merely draws a line under the nullity of meaning.[33]

Like all other Japanese signs analysed by Barthes, haiku writing is therefore exempted from meaning; it triggers but at the same time resists interpretation: 'The haiku wakens desire [...]. While being quite intelligible, the haiku means nothing, and it is by this double condition that it seems open to meaning in a particularly available, serviceable way.'[34] It is worth noting of course that Japanese amateurs or specialists of haikus would probably not agree with Barthes's definition of this type of poems, that he associates with Zen Buddhism and more specifically with the notion of 'satori'. In fact, as he acknowledges himself, *his* haiku – that is, what he refers to when he uses this term – does not only designate the traditional poetic genre, but it encapsulates the very essence of Japanese art and aesthetic sensibility: 'Neither describing nor defining, the haiku (as I shall finally name any discontinuous feature, any event of Japanese life as it offers itself to my reading), the haiku diminishes to the point of pure and sole designation.'[35] According to Barthes, the haiku has the property to designate its object without describing nor defining it, that is to say without locking it in the realm of meaning. Naturally, the haiku always has a meaning which can be understood by the reader (i.e. it is and remains 'intelligible'), but Barthes claims this level of signification is of secondary importance, almost insignificant – and finally 'emptied', exempted from or of meaning. In his reading of Japan, all signs are treated as pure designations, like the haiku; the pleasure they give is of an emotional nature, and does not require any interpretation or analysis.

33   Barthes, *Empire of Signs*, p. 76.
34   *Ibid.*, p. 69.
35   *Ibid.*, p. 83.

In conclusion, Barthes identified in Japan a specific structure of signification which tends to empty or exempt signs from their meaning – a
structure redoubled by his position as a Western traveller not familiar
with Japanese culture and not understanding Japanese language. His very
personal response to this country offered him a way to escape what he
perceived as the Western tyranny of meaning and logic, and considerably
helped him in his search for new modes of expression and reception in his
late work. As he himself lucidly observes, 'Japan has starred him with any
number of "flashes"; or, better still, Japan has afforded him a situation of
writing. This situation is the very one in which a certain disturbance of the
person occurs, a subversion of earlier readings.'[36]

'Un-countried' in Japan: Chris Marker's *Sans Soleil* and *Le Dépays*

Unlike Barthes who only made in total three relatively short visits to
Japan, Chris Marker stayed in the Archipelago for longer periods of time
and even considered it to be his *dépays* (literally, his 'un-country'), that is,
his second – and yet foreign – home. Although he travelled extensively
around the world, this country has been a central and continued inspiration for his work as a film director, writer and photographer since the
first stay he made there in 1964 to film the Tokyo Olympic Games, during
which he also shot *Le Mystère Koumiko* (*The Koumiko Mystery*, completed in 1965).[37] This forty-six minute film portrays Kumiko Muraoka, a
young girl in her twenties Marker met while documenting the Olympics,
and who speaks to him about Japan, being Japanese and her unique perspective on life. As the narrative voice suggests at the very beginning of
the movie, ' "Japan is all around her." It pervades every image. Traditional,
modern, folkloric, surprising, it is everywhere; it is visible but it resists

36   *Ibid.*, p. 4.
37   Chris Marker, *Le Mystère Koumiko*, documentary film, 46 mins (Paris: La
      Sofra, 1965).

at the same time any attempt to get closer and to understand it.'[38] This mixture of fascination, mystery and opacity is characteristic of Marker's stance towards Japan, a country he wants to show based on his chance encounters, without explaining or analysing it. The documentary but also very personal feel of *Le Mystère Koumiko* can also be found in *Sunless*, undoubtedly his most important film focusing on Japanese culture and society. However, *Sunless* has a greater fictional dimension and is therefore more difficult to classify in terms of genre. Its main protagonist, Sandor Krasna, can be considered as Marker's avatar since we learn he is a film director travelling all around the world; his commentaries, reported in the form of letters read by a female narrator, develop a reflection on the nature of recorded images (movies, photos, TV footages ...), memory and history. This film is for a large part made up of the images that Krasna is said to have filmed in Japan, Africa and Iceland, but some scenes have also been borrowed from other documentaries and movies such as Alfred Hitchcock's *Vertigo*.

At the beginning of *Sunless*, we are told that in one of his letters the fictional director evoked in relation to Japan 'these simple joys he had never felt: of returning to a country, a house, a family home.'[39] Like Barthes, Marker tended to emphasise in his depiction of this faraway, unfamiliar country *par excellence* images of everyday life, banal scenes and ordinary objects encountered randomly. While the author of *Empire of Signs* focused on food, packages or city maps, Marker shows in his film pictures of ceremonies in temples and of people travelling – and sleeping – on trains or walking in the bustling streets of Tokyo. These images are merely juxtaposed without apparent logical link, or rather following the principle of free association which is largely driven by the unconscious and also reflects the way memory works. The film commentary regularly underlines this singular structure, announcing for instance a new sequence seemingly unrelated with a rhetorical question: 'by the way, did you know that they are emus in the Ile de France?' As a movie maker, Marker refuses to create

38 *Ibid.*, my translation.
39 Chris Marker, *Sunless*, documentary film, 100 mins (Paris: Argos Film, 1983); the text of the film commentary can be found on the following website: <https://www.markertext.com/sans_soleil.htm>.

a story and to convey clear messages, his only ambition being to show images and to present *his* Japan to the viewers. This is what is implied by the following comment: 'if they don't see happiness in the picture, at least they'll see the black'.

Based on these guiding principles, Marker does not attempt to control or influence the reception of images in the narrator's commentary. This is in line with Barthes's foreword in *Empire of Signs*, which states that 'The text does not "gloss" the images, which do not "illustrate" the text. [...] Text and image, interlacing, seek to ensure the circulation of these signifiers: body, face, writing; and in them, the retreat of signs.'[40] Marker concurs with Barthes's refusal to impose a meaning to the Japanese signifiers he has chosen to show, which is confirmed by the incipit of *Le Dépays*, a largely unknown photo-text on Japan he published in 1982, one year before *Sunless* was released:[41]

> The text doesn't comment on the images any more than the images illustrate the text. They are two sequences that clearly cross and signal to each other, but which it would be pointlessly exhausting to collate. One should therefore accept them in their disorder, simplicity and division in two, as with everything else in Japan.[42]

This foreword obviously reads like a rewriting of – and tribute to – the opening page of *Empire of Signs*, with respect to the image-text relation in particular.[43] Following in Barthes's footsteps in his response to Japan, it is not surprising that Marker tends to emphasise the banality, simplicity and fragility of the scenes he shot and assembled. In this respect, the commentary of the film suggests with reference to Sandor Krasna: 'He liked the fragility of those moments suspended in time. Those memories whose only function had been to leave behind nothing but memories. He

---

40   Barthes, *Empire of Signs*, p. xi.
41   Chris Marker, *Le Dépays* (Paris: Herscher, 1982).
42   Translated by Catherine Lupton in *Chris Marker: Memories of the Future* (London: Reaktion Books, 2005), p. 62. Lupton adds that 'Marker's advice to the reader of *Le Dépays* could equally apply to the book's relationship to *Sunless*' (*ibid.*).
43   In *Le Dépays*, Marker presents *Empire of Signs* as one of the three major essays written to date on Japan, along with Kenji Tokitsu's *La Voie du karaté* (1979) and Satoshi Kamata's *Japon, l'envers du miracle* (1982).

wrote: I've been round the world several times and now only banality still interests me.'

By evoking memories 'whose only function is to leave memories', Marker does not only emulate Barthes here in his attempt to escape the Western obsession to give meaning to everything and to go beyond literal and factual content; he also praises features that he perceives as pertaining to the essence of Japanese sensibility, and which guide his selection of images and commentary. Indeed, a few minutes later in the film, the narrator refers to Sei Shōnagon, the author of *Makura no Sōshi* (*The Pillow Book*), a collection of daily observations, short stories and poetry that constitutes one of Marker's key sources of inspiration on Japan. Sei Shōnagon was a lady in waiting to Princess Sadako at the beginning of the eleventh century, in the Heian period, during which – as one of Sandor Krasna's letters explains:

> the emperor's court had become nothing more than a place of intrigues and intellectual games. But by learning to draw a sort of melancholy comfort from the contemplation of the tiniest things this small group of idlers left a mark on Japanese sensibility much deeper than the mediocre thundering of the politicians. Shōnagon had a passion for lists: the list of 'elegant things', 'distressing things', or even of 'things not worth doing'. One day she got the idea of drawing up a list of 'things that quicken the heart'. Not a bad criterion I realise when I'm filming; I bow to the economic miracle, but what I want to show you are the neighbourhood celebrations.[44]

These remarks clearly have a self-referential dimension and are key to understand Marker's aesthetic project and choice of images in *Sunless*. On the one hand, Shōnagon's meticulous style of observation, paying attention to seemingly insignificant details and at times voyeuristic, appears to have influenced his approach as a filmmaker in the movie. But perhaps more importantly, this reference to a monument of Japanese traditional literature and culture explains Marker's anti-touristic enterprise and focus on trivial, everyday matters off the beaten tracks. His subjective take on *his* Japan is thus justified and anchored in Japanese artistic tradition and sensibility.

This is later confirmed in the film by another allusion to *The Pillow Book*, again in one of Krasna's letters read by the narrator:

44   Marker, *Sunless*.

I thought of Shōnagon's list, of all those signs one has only to name to quicken the heart, just name. To us, a sun is not quite a sun unless it's radiant, and a spring not quite a spring unless it is limpid. Here to place adjectives would be so rude as leaving price tags on purchases. Japanese poetry never modifies [qualifies]. There is a way of saying boat, rock, mist, frog, crow, hail, heron, chrysanthemum, that includes them all.[45]

The essentialising dichotomy between Japan ('here') and the West ('us') is here reminiscent of Barthes's approach throughout *Empire of Signs*. But these comments are also close to his definition of the haiku, that Krasna's 'moments suspended in time' evoked earlier were already alluding to. As we have seen, the haiku tends for Barthes to resist adjectivisation and commentary, and to produce a form of plain poetic expression that reaches a kind of absolute, without the need to qualify the objects or feelings being described:

> The haiku's task is to achieve exemption from meaning within a perfectly readerly discourse (a contradiction denied to Western art, which can contest meaning only by rendering its discourse incomprehensible) [...]; insignificant nonetheless, it resists us, finally loses the adjectives which a moment before we had bestowed upon it, and enters into that suspension of meaning which to us is the strangest thing of all, since it makes impossible the most ordinary exercise of our language, which is commentary.[46]

This helps us to better understand the mode of expression and haiku-like, fragmentary form used in *Sunless*, which is after all nothing other than a filmic list of 'things that quicken the heart', inspired by the spirit of Japanese traditional literature. To borrow the words of Marker's commentary, this film is made up of 'pictures that are less deceptive [...] than those you see on television. At least they proclaim themselves to be what they are: images, not the portable and compact form of an already inaccessible reality.'[47] As we have seen in Krasna's letters, a memory's only function is to leave memories, images should be received as such, and by extension, Barthes and Marker's respective works on – and inspired by – Japan can be considered first and foremost as an invitation to take signs for what

45   *Ibid.*
46   Barthes, *Empire of Signs*, p. 81.
47   Marker, *Sunless.*

they are, be they texts, images or otherwise; before potentially referring to another reality, they are a reality in themselves and should be enjoyed for their sensual dimension as signifiers. Although the meaning of signs can change depending on contexts, signifiers remain and resist in a form of combined plainness and stubbornness exemplified by what Barthes called an exemption from meaning. This is well illustrated by *Empire of Signs* and *Sunless* which detach Japanese signifiers from their usual context of reception, and insert them in complex assemblages of signs. For instance, images from 1960s events such as the violent protests against the construction of Tokyo Narita airport – addressed by both French authors – start to lose their political meaning when they are treated by the synthesiser of Hayao Yamaneko, another avatar of the film director in *Sunless*, who transforms them in digital patches of colour. Marker therefore agrees with the claim Barthes made in his *Mythologies* and later works that history itself is a cultural product, a partly fictional and always evolving discourse, only deceptively naturalised and essentialised.

The peculiar approach to Japan in *Sunless* is enlightened in many ways by Marker's 1982 photo-text *Le Dépays* (*The Un-country*), a neologism clearly expressing his dis-orienting experience while in the Archipelago but also his profound attachment to this country. In the short essay that opens the book, he writes in this respect:

> If you want to get to know Japan you may just as well invent it. Once received ideas have been left behind, once the received idea to dissipate received ideas has been bypassed, mathematically everyone has the same chance [of getting to know Japan] – and how much time spared![48]

In other words, according to Marker, trying to avoid clichés and stereotypes about Japan is a cliché in itself, and just another way to be mistaken about this country – of course, one could read this statement as an unconvincing excuse, but the author's point here is that his work is of a subjective nature and does not attempt to produce a discourse of knowledge. At the end of the same text, he adds, still referring to Japan – or rather *his* Japan: 'Such is my imagined country, a country that I totally

---

48   Marker, *Le Dépays*, n.p.; my translation.

invented, totally invested, a country that surpasses me so much that it becomes disorientation itself. My un-country.'[49] This explicitation by Marker of the title of his book can be directly related to what Barthes claims at the beginning of *Empire of Signs*: 'I can also – though in no way claiming to represent or to analyse reality itself [...] – isolate somewhere in the world (faraway) a certain number of features [...], and out of these features deliberately form a system. It is this system which I shall call: Japan.'[50] Barthes and Marker both adopt the same nonchalant attitude towards Japan and roam the streets of Tokyo and other cities like the Surrealists used to in search for accidental signs and events, for chance encounters; they celebrate the magic of everyday life in Japan, or what they perceive as such, to a large extent because it appears fundamentally mysterious to them. As Catherine Lupton rightly noted in her essay entitled *Chris Marker: Memories of the Future*,

> Japan, in Marker's estimation, is a country that obligingly refuses to make sense, forcing the visitor to accept everything in its 'disorder, simplicity and division in two', as he puts it in *Le Dépays*, and basically to make it up as he goes along.[51]

Barthes says nothing other when he claims in *Empire of Signs* that 'Japan has starred him with any number of "flashes".[52]

As such, Japan – or the imagined, invented country, the Other *par excellence* – becomes a kind of screen onto which Barthes and Marker can project their obsessions, fantasies and desires.[53] But in their case, what

---

49   *Ibid.*, my translation.
50   Barthes, *Empire of Signs*, p. 3.
51   Lupton, *Chris Marker*, p. 99.
52   Barthes, *Empire of Signs*, p. 4.
53   As Olaf Möller rightly noted, 'Although Westerners attribute a high level of truthfulness to Marker's Japan (especially as seen in *Sans soleil*), in essence it's a fictional ghost world, a looking-glass country' (Olaf Möller, 'Chris Marker: Ghost World. Japan Through the Looking Glass', *Film Comment*, July/August 2003, pp. 35–7, (p. 36)). In a recent article, Brian Howell proposed a similar but more nuanced view: 'the Japan that Marker the filmmaker and person makes available to us is both not completely real in the sense that not every Japanese person will recognise the Japan that she sees in the film as representative of the Japan that she knows. Yet, it is real enough to provide the viewer with insights into the essence of both the Japan of

is projected is precisely a fantasy of the everyday, of the banal and the insignificant, Japan being traditionally associated in the japoniste and neo-japoniste imaginary with the everyday – often via stereotypical representations found in nineteenth-century *japonaiseries* and via the diffusion of a simplified Zen culture after the Second World War. In this respect, Michael Sheringham, for example, claimed that 'in *L'Empire des signes* the everyday is called Japan'.[54]

In conclusion, Barthes and Marker both attempted in their respective works to encapsulate what they thought were crucial features of Japanese cultural and artistic sensibility, that is, an acute awareness of the fragility of meaning and an aesthetic appreciation of everydayness.[55] Confronted with an unfamiliar culture, unknown codes and signs, they decided to focus on a series of 'things that quicken the heart', and abandoned themselves to the pleasure of signifiers – especially visual. However misled they might have been, their reflection on the nature of signs and singular responses to Japanese culture have had a strong and lasting influence on their contemporaries, their emphasis on the pleasure of 'Texte Japon' (or Japan-as-text) explaining to a large extent their appeal to readers and viewers over several decades, in the West and beyond. Despite the errors and stereotypes conveyed, they made an important point concerning the reception of artistic and cultural signs, which cannot be reduced to their significations – allowing

---

today and of the past' (Brian Howell, 'Chris Marker's Real and Unreal Japan – *Sans Soleil* as Intercultural Document', *Language, Culture, and Communication*, vol. 9 (2017), pp. 149–59 (p. 159)).

54   Michael Sheringham, *Everyday Life: Theories and Practices from Surrealism to the Present* (Oxford: Oxford University Press, 2006), p. 197. This is how Sheringham analyses this phenomenon: 'Barthes's 1966–68 encounter with Japan intensified his fascination with the everyday, hatching a number of notions and forms that would remain "live" for the rest of his career. In this further evolution and re-evaluation the ethical, existential, and hedonistic dimensions of Barthes's passion for the processes of signification fully emerge. And from this point the word "vie" will play a significant role in his discourse' (*ibid.*, p. 197).

55   For more on this, see Yuriko Saito's *Everyday Aesthetics* (Oxford: Oxford University Press, 2010) and *Aesthetics of the Familiar: Everyday Life and World-Making* (Oxford: Oxford University Press, 2017).

in themselves a pleasure of deciphering, decoding meaning – and should be enjoyed first as pleasurable signifiers.

Empire of Signs and Sunless both have a positive, euphoric and hedonist approach to their object, but also a more negative, critical dimension. Indeed, Barthes and Marker found in Japan a 'dépays', an utopic space and faraway land compared to which they could criticise various aspects and values they disliked in Western civilisation. It is in this perspective that their predilection for the everyday, for insignificant details of daily life in Japan can be understood as a way of countering the dominance of ideological superstructures in French social and artistic circles in the 1960s and 1970s (e.g. Existentialism, Marxism, Structuralism ...). The pleasure of signifiers has therefore a neutralising function for them, and serves various strategic goals beyond the mere question of textual or visual enjoyment. As Forsdick puts it, this allows Barthes 'to decentre and destabilize the sense-making strategies provided by his home culture' in Empire of Signs, a fantasy world in which an 'exemption from meaning' has been achieved.[56] This fantasy, largely shared by Marker, is combined in the works considered in this chapter with an aestheticentric tendency to praise Japanese minimalism – as it is perceived in the eyes of Western authors – but also the figure of the neutral via Japan and more specifically Zen culture.[57] Such an approach can be described as reductionist, essentialising and de-historicising, and by extension as neo-japoniste or orientalist, but one should not only emphasise the limits but also the merits of Barthes and Marker's endeavour; in this respect, the self-reflexive and at times ironical dimension of their photo-text and film should not be overlooked. They precisely use the cognitive and sensitive gap between different media – that is, still or moving images and spoken or written words – to create distance from their object and spark the critical reflection of their readers/viewers, thus avoiding a primary form of exoticism. Both authors are all too aware of these issues as their forewords indicate, and Barthes in particular had already expressed concerns on this point in his Mythologies, in the last footnote of which he confesses: 'Even here, in these mythologies, I have used trickery: finding

56   Forsdick, '(In)connaissance de l'Asie', p. 70.
57   See my note 19 referring to Kōjin Karatani's definition of 'aestheticentrism'.

it painful constantly to work on the evaporation of reality, I have started to make it excessively dense, and to discover in it a surprising compactness which I savoured with delight.'[58] By organising in *Empire of Signs* an 'evaporation of reality' – the 'real' Japan – and savouring 'excessively dense' signifiers of 'a surprising compactness', Barthes eventually assumed a somewhat paradoxical position in and in relation to this country, a position that could be described to use an expression from *The Pleasure of the Text* as 'doubly perverse'; like Marker in *Sunless* and *Le Dépays*, he enjoys the destruction of the Western values he condemns but relishes at the same time in the pleasure of Japanese signs – seeking thus both pleasure and bliss in *his* Japan:

> He [the subject] simultaneously and contradictorily participates in the profound hedonism of all culture (which permeates him quietly under the cover of an *art de vivre* shared by the old books) and in the destruction of that culture: he enjoys the consistency of his selfhood (that is his pleasure) and seeks its loss (that is his bliss). He is a subject split twice over, doubly perverse.[59]

58   Roland Barthes, *Mythologies*, trans. by Richard Howard and Annette Lavers (New York: Hill and Wang, 2013), p. 158, note 30.

59   Barthes, *The Pleasure of the Text*, p. 14.

ANDY STAFFORD

7   The Barthesian 'Double Grasp' in Japan Reading as Undialectical Writing[1]

In memory of Toshitaka Ida

Introduction

> Good prose is like a windowpane.
>
> – George Orwell[2]

If we can think of pleasure in Roland Barthes's writing taken *in* writing, it must be considered as born from a necessity. Though he seemed to take most pleasure in his writing of Japan, in *L'Empire des signes* (1970), it involved an analysis that invited a level of complexity which was at times dizzying.[3] As the Moroccan critic and friend, Abdelkébir Khatibi, suggested with regard to *L'Empire des signes*: 'Roland Barthes se situe, il l'a répété, entre celui qui écrit qu'il écrit et celui qui écrit qu'il analyse' [Roland Barthes locates himself, as he has often said, between the person

---

1   Thanks to Emmanuel Lozerand and the participants in the seminar series on *L'Empire de signes* at INALCO (Paris) who kindly listened to and commented on a first, French version of this chapter, which was then rewritten in English, by a strange fate, in Shanghai.

2   George Orwell, 'Why I Write' (1946), <http://orwell.ru/library/essays/wiw/english/e_wiw>.

3   '[W]hen I wrote that book I felt a pleasure unmixed with anxiety, untainted by the *imago*'; see Barthes, *The Grain of the Voice. Interviews 1962–1980*, trans. by Linda Coverdale (New York: Hill & Wang, 1985), p. 229.

who writes that they are writing, and who writes that they are analysing].[4] It is this double seeing, this in-between two activities, that we will investigate here as a potential source of pleasure.

Much is made of this notion of multi-tasking, and its practical application in twenty-first-century life. Yet, in visual terms, Barthes seemed persuaded – at least in 'Le mythe, aujourd'hui' in 1957 – that humans could not see two things at once:

> [S]i je suis en auto et que je regarde le paysage à travers la vitre, je puis accommoder à volonté sur le paysage ou sur la vitre : tantôt je saisirai la présence de la vitre et la distance du paysage ; tantôt au contraire la transparence de la vitre et la profondeur du paysage ; mais le résultat de cette alternance sera constant : la vitre me sera à la fois présente et vide, le paysage me sera à la fois irréel et plein.

> [If I am in a car and I look at the scenery through the window, I can at will focus on the scenery or on the windowpane. At one moment I grasp the presence of the glass and the distance of the landscape; at another, on the contrary, the transparence [sic] of the glass and the depth of the landscape; but the result of this alternation is constant: the glass is at once present and empty to me, and the landscape unreal and full.][5]

Pessimistic as they may seem as to the inability of humans to grasp two things at once, the aim of this chapter is to show the opposite in Barthes's work. The 'double grasp', as we shall see, involves the pleasure of reading, but also then writing.[6] However, the pleasure of the 'double grasp' is also

---

4   Abdelkébir Khatibi, 'Le Japon de Barthes', in *Figures de l'étranger dans la littérature française* (Paris: Denoël, 1987), p. 63 (my translation).

5   Roland Barthes, 'Le mythe, aujourd'hui' (1957), in *Mythologies* (Paris: Seuil, 1970), p. 209, republished in *Œuvres complètes*, ed. by Éric Marty, 5 vols (Paris: Seuil, 2002), henceforth referenced as *OC* followed by volume number; *OC* I 836; 'Myth Today' in *A Barthes Reader*, ed. by Susan Sontag (New York: Hill and Wang, 1982), p. 110.

6   On optical metaphors in Barthes's writing, see Marie-Jeanne Zenetti 'Transparence, opacité, matité dans l'œuvre de Roland Barthes, du *Degré zéro de l'écriture* à *L'Empire des signes*', *Appareil*, n°7 (2011): <https://journals.openedition.org/appareil/1201>. Barthes had already seen a 'double grasp' at work in the research of André Ombredane (1898–1958) involving comparative psychological tests on Belgian and Congolese students, using films by Jean Painlevé and Jacques Cousteau; in 'Littérature littérale', citing Edgar Morin's work, Barthes considered this 'expérience

in its very deconstruction. In what Barthes calls a 'new dialectic', the very notion and practice of the 'double grasp' will be shown to undergo a 'mutation'; and it is in his 1970 essay *L'Empire des signes* that we will trace its trajectory. In his study of modern forms of observation, Jonathan Crary, sees the nineteenth century – and not at all the *camera obscura* of the seventeenth and eighteenth centuries – as the key to modern tropes of seeing.[7] In parallel with Crary's bold assertion, we trace the 'double grasp' to Barthes's 1954 presentation of the writings of the nineteenth-century historian Jules Michelet. This raises a first question: why look in *L'Empire des signes* for examples of the double grasp?

From Creative Criticism to the 'Undialectical'

'[D]eviens, en écriture, *quelqu'un.*'
[Become, in writing, *someone*]

– Roland Barthes[8]

There are many candidates that display a 'double grasp' in Barthes's major works. In *Le Degré zéro de l'écriture* in 1953, we can already see a 'double grasp' at work in the way it argues for both a literary 'responsabilité' and, at the same time, a political form of *engagement*. Otherwise, we could look to *Mythologies* – despite the denial of (visual) multi-tasking that we saw above in 'Le mythe, aujourd'hui' – in which we certainly can see a 'double grasp' at work in the hyper-focused analysis that Barthes applies

---

    ethnologique d'Ombredane' to be indicative of the conditioning taking place in the European 'civilisations d'âme'; see *OC* I 821 n2, *OC* II 779 and 914 n1, and *OC* V 828; see Edgar Morin, *Cinéma ou l'homme imaginaire* (Paris: Minuit, 1956), p. 115.

7   Jonathan Crary, *Techniques of the Observer. On Vision and Modernity in the Nineteenth Century* (Cambridge, MA: MIT Press, 1992); my thanks to Magali Nachtergael for this reference.

8   Roland Barthes, *Carnets du voyage en Chine* [1974] (Paris: Christian Bourgois éditeur, 2009), p. 21.

to both meaning and the real of an object, written using a dialectical suppleness.[9] Then, we might suggest taking a look at his essay that caused an academic and literary uproar in 1963, *Sur Racine*; its analysis of theatrical narration style displays a structural attentiveness to the story as, simultaneously, both an anthropological and an unconscious category; and Racine's theatre is deemed one which is both intransitive and excluding of mediation: 'le monde racinien est un monde à deux termes' [the Racinian world is a world of two terms], declared Barthes; 'son statut est paradoxal, non dialectique: le troisième terme manque' [its status is paradoxical, not dialectical: the third term is missing].[10] This critique of Racinian theatre dovetailed with a well-read treatise on the dialectic during the 1960s and 1970s, *Dialectique du concret* by Karel Kosik, which was published in French in 1970.[11] Just as Kosik underlines the transformational and transitive dimension of the dialectic, so, as we shall see, much of the analysis in *L'Empire des signes* is concerned with agency, the doing and the transforming of the everyday world. Indeed, transitivity and mediation will become key values for Barthes's Japan and the 'new dialectic'. But first we quickly survey other examples of 'double grasp' in the years before the visits to Japan.

In the first half of the 1960s, we could have consulted *Éléments de sémiologie* (1964), where semiology is taken as a classic example of 'double grasp', with the division between signifier and signified. Likewise, Barthes's very precise work on fashion across the sixties, in *Système de la mode* (1967) and in other texts, takes women's clothing and fashion styles both as 'written' clothing (already a type of 'double grasp'), only then also for Barthes to insert his own analysis within a methodological relativity that underlines the power of the 'detail' (brooch, bracelet, button, etc.), a complexity that pertains in any type of *combinatoire*; and this is all presented as if it were a *prosopopeia* of Woman in the middle of persuading herself about her next

9   See Andy Stafford, 'Dialectics of Form(s) in Roland Barthes's *Mythologies*', *Nottingham French Studies*, vol. 47, n°2 (2008), pp. 6–18.

10   *OC* II 97; Roland Barthes, *On Racine* (1963), trans. by Richard Howard (Berkeley/Los Angeles: University of California Press, 1992), p. 49.

11   Karel Kosik, *La Dialectique du concret*, trans. from the German by Roger Dangeville (Paris: Maspero, 1970).

fashion purchase.[12] Finally, published in 1970, the same year as *L'Empire des signes*, *S/Z* could be shown to display a 'double grasp', as it reads and rewrites Balzac's disturbing and disruptive story, *Sarrasine*, using a method that Barthes calls 'stéréographique': 'esquisser l'espace stéréographique d'une écriture (qui sera ici écriture classique, lisible)' [sketch the stereographic space of writing (which will here be a classic, readerly writing)].[13]

However, in this chapter we will persist in the use of *L'Empire des signes* to analyse the double grasp. This is above all for writerly reasons, as well as readerly ones. Firstly, written in Morocco in 1969, after his second visit, the same year, to Japan, it is not a coincidence that *L'Empire des signes* published in a collection called 'Les sentiers de la création'.[14] Furthermore, it may be surprising to underline, as Éric Marty has done, that *L'Empire des signes* is actually Barthes's very first 'freely' written piece of his career.[15] As journalist, critic, researcher and teacher, Barthes never published anything in book form, before *L'Empire des signes*, that did not exist already in one form or another.[16] *S/Z* emerges from the seminar notes that he wrote for his students at the EPHE in 1968 and 1969; *Sur Racine* is a collection of reviews and articles published in a variety of journals between 1959 and 1962 – *Mythologies*, *Michelet* and *Le Degré zéro de l'écriture*, likewise. The only exception is *Critique et vérité* (1966) – however, if *Critique et vérité* seems to come from nowhere in terms of previous texts and writings, the essay is written as a direct response to the shrill criticisms of *Sur Racine* by Sorbonne professor Raymond Picard, thereby suggesting, strongly, a jousting – rather than a creative – type of essay. Thus, we could indeed say that *L'Empire des signes* is Barthes's first real, proper creation; and its pure

12   See Olivier Burgelin, 'Le double système de la mode', *l'Arc*, n°56 (1974), pp. 8–16 – republished in Roland Barthes, *Le Bleu est à la mode cette année. Et autres articles* (Paris: Institut Français de la Mode, 2001) –, especially p. 12.

13   Roland Barthes, *S/Z* (Paris: Seuil, 1970), p. 21; trans. by Richard Miller (New York: Hill & Wang, 1974), p. 15.

14   Claude Coste, *Roland Barthes, ou l'art du détour* (Paris: Hermann, 2016), p. 88.

15   Éric Marty, 'Présentation', *OC* III 15.

16   However, 'Leçon d'écriture', published in *Tel Quel* (n°34) in Summer 1968 (*OC* III 33–9), is a prelude to 'Les trois écritures' in *L'Empire des signes* though it is a relatively small section of the essay.

creativity relates to the creative criticism that Barthes is developing between *Critique et vérité* in 1966 and *S/Z* in 1970. It would be ill-advised therefore if we excluded *L'Empire des signes* from this 'mutation'.

There is a final reason to look for 'double grasp' in *L'Empire des signes*. In his 1968 piece on Bunraku called (appropriately enough for us here) 'Leçon d'écriture', Barthes suggested that the dialectical principle of contradiction weighs much less heavily on Japanese thought:

> L'Antithèse est une figure privilégiée de notre culture […]. De ces contraires, de cette antonymie qui règle toute notre morale du discours, le Bunraku se moque.
>
> [Antithesis is a privileged figure of our culture. Bunraku cares nothing for these contraries, for this antonymy that regulates our whole morality of discourse][17]

This brief disqualification of the antithetical will become, by the time of writing *L'Empire des signes*, a wider consideration of the dialectic in both Japanese and Western culture. Barthesian creative criticism, by the time of the late 1960s, and especially in the aftermath of May '68, begins to develop a dialectical formalism, a hyper-dialectics – albeit 'undialectical' – that recognises that 'double grasp', in its act of apprehending the world, needs to be confronted with writerly creativity. The resulting complexity might be explored if we extrapolate Barthes's window/countryside metaphor cited above.

I am writing these words sitting in a train and, sometimes, looking out of the window. What Barthes does not mention in his window/countryside metaphor is that the countryside beyond the window is moving; or rather, I and the window are both in motion; and this is a good image for what we will suggest concerning *L'Empire des signes*. Not only is it difficult to accommodate in our vision both window and countryside; but also, we are often looking through a window at a countryside that is moving. This idea suggests then a further level of complexity to our discussion of Barthes's essay 'on' Japan; partly because, not only is the essay not a scientific presentation of Japanese culture (so it is not 'on' Japan), nor is it 'about' France or

17   *OC* III 34, trans. by Stephen Heath, in *Image-Music-Text* (Glasgow: Fontana, 1977), p. 171.

Europe (the 'West'). Instead, *L'Empire des signes* is all these things, except that it is (also, via) a 'stereographic' writing 'on' writing.

If the levels of vision now seem dizzying in their number, interaction and complexity – not just the countryside (and which we cannot see at the same time as the window) and its movement but also the mediation of writing language introduced into Barthes's multi-optics – then this is appropriate to the philosophical and theoretical level at which his creative criticism is operating. Introducing a further dimension is part of a complexity that illustrates well what Barthes the writer feels up against. Complexity is also a simple definition (if the oxymoron be excused!) of the dialectic; and with Barthes this complexity is related to the window, but augmented, complexified, by the fact that he then moves to write this 'double grasp', this visual multi-tasking.

In this optic of the complex, the struggle before the window – between on the one hand a semiology, and an ideology on the other – is confronted by turn, as if in a game of chess with three boards on different levels (famously played by Spock on the American TV 1960s futuristic series *Star Trek*) by another 'double grasp'; that of a form of writing, practised either by a Writer, or by an Author. In a footnote in his *Arguments* essay in 1960, 'Écrivains et écrivants', having set out the *non*-dialectical nature of language and at the same time the injunction that we should be dialectical, Barthes made a stark suggestion: 'l'écrivain se dialectise, il ne dialectise pas le monde' [the author dialecticizes himself, he does not dialecticize the world].[18] In other words, the grasp of the real is not able to accommodate window and countryside simultaneously; and, at the same time, this very non-accommodation must become part of the writing. Semiology against ideology on the one side must also confront *both* 'écrire pour rien' *and* 'écrire pour une cause' on the other, in a *chassé-croisé* whose proportions and consequences are multiple. If this is the undialectical, it must not be confused with adialectical or anti-dialectical; but precisely as the exact

18   Roland Barthes, 'Écrivains et écrivants' (1960), in *Essais critiques* (Paris: Seuil, 1964), p. 150 note 5 (*A Barthes Reader*, p. 188, though a sentence is missing in the English translation).

opposite of non-dialectical. Indeed, there is debate rumbling in Barthes's oeuvre towards Marx and questions of agency.

In 'Le mythe, aujourd'hui', as a response to Marx's cherry-tree, presented in *The German Ideology* as an object that is always 'political' and therefore 'mediated' (132), Barthes invokes the wood-cutter who is described in 'Le mythe, aujourd'hui' as the only possible actor able to 'act' directly (on) the object by being outside of the intransitivity of language.[19] This critique of Marx leads in 1971 to Barthes's view that, even in Marx, written language is 'undialectical', only ever 'paradoxical', not a dialectic but a spiral, not a synthesis but a 'chain of discourses'?[20] If Marx cannot use language transitively, then no-one can, was perhaps Barthes's implication.[21] That, in good Barthesian style, now becomes the challenge in *L'Empire des signes*: to write dialectically, but in a 'double grasp'. In other words, there is a sort of dialectic in Barthes's work, and which must be traced in writing itself, that is, the *written* grasp and not just its prior, visual counterpart.[22]

19   *OC* I 855–6 (*A Barthes Reader*, pp. 132–4).

20   *OC* III 894–5 ('Writers, Intellectuals, Teachers', in *A Barthes Reader*, p. 388).

21   On the undialectical in the early – Hegelian – Marx, see Jean-François Gava, *Contrariété sans dialectique. Logique et politique hégéliennes face à la critique sociale marxienne* (Paris: L'Harmattan, 2011). It is also the early Nietzsche of *The Birth of Tragedy*, as Barthes appreciated in his 1941 postgraduate thesis: 'Dans les incantations, ivresse et dialectique se confondent; ou plutôt, c'est à tort que nous les avons dissociées avant de les confondre. Elles ne font qu'une, dès l'origine – témoignant – pour s'être conciliées avant de naître –, (sic) du miracle unique dont les Grecs font encore à présent jusque sur nous, (sic) rayonner le prestige et le mystère. Elles consacrent avec éclat l'identification de Dionysos et d'Apollon, et montrent qu'il ne faut pas considérer cette union comme une réconciliation ou une synthèse tardive, mais comme une confusion d'origine et de nature'; see Barthes, 'Évocations et incantations ...' (Archives Roland Barthes, BNF, NAF 28630), p. 138.

22   Abdelkébir Khatibi's 'double critique', his citing of *L'Empire des signes* as a non-logocentric ethnography in *Blessure du nom propre* (Paris: Denoël, 1974), p. 64, and the central notion of 'dédoublement' in the *Mémoire tatouée* (Paris: Denoël, 1971) – especially the last chapter, 'Double contre double' – might all be considered as examples of 'double grasp'; on this, see Andrea Flores Khalil, 'A Writing in Points: Autobiography and the Poetics of the Tattoo', *Journal of North African Studies*, vol. 8, n°2 (2003), which sees the tattoo as releasing script from the antagonism of the dialectic.

Essayism *versus* the Impressionistic?

This written 'grasp' is historically situated. 1969 and 1970 are the post-68, but not quite the moment in which Maoism would, briefly, tempt Barthes between 1971 and 1973, a brief moment that had all but ended by the time of the famous visit with *Tel Quel* to China in 1974. The let-down that was 1968 for everyone in the years following, Barthes included, led, at worst, to a decadence; at best, to a realisation of why May 1968 had not won: everything – albeit changed, modified, 'muté' – went back to how it was before. As Barthes put it succinctly in an interview in May 1970 on *L'Empire des signes*: 'Il faut vivre', he declared to Raymond Bellour in *Les Lettres françaises*, 'dans l'inhabitable' [we have to live amid the unlivable].[23]

Given this context, it is difficult not to be frustrated by any reading of Barthes's essay that is falsely simple, simplistic, disingenuous. Recent, supple readings of *L'Empire des signes* do exist – for example, the 'double regard gai' neatly explored by Magali Nachtergael.[24] But hostile readings have begun to surface. To put it in more pessimistic, negative terms, if the double dimension of the 'double grasp' – complexified – is ignored, if we look only at the 'countryside' of *L'Empire des signes*, without looking also at the window, we risk a 'mono' (as opposed to a double) 'grasp'.

For example, in a rather puerile book by arch critic of his, *Roland Barthes, Grotesque de notre temps*, René Pommier maintains, for example, that Barthes's disdain in 1970 for 'le signe tristement alourdi de son signifié' had overlooked something simple: the fact that a sign without a signified 'n'est plus rien'.[25] Only for Pommier then to concentrate on what he calls

23   *OC* III 670 (*The Grain of the Voice*, p. 87).
24   Magali Nachtergael, 'Barthes à l'aune des Queer et Visual studies', in Jean-Pierre Bertrand (ed.), *Roland Barthes: continuités. Colloque de Cerisy 2016* (Paris: Bourgois, 2017), pp. 417–36 (pp. 425–6).
25   René Pommier, *Roland Barthes, Grotesque de notre temps. Grotesque de tous les temps* (Paris: Kimé, 2017), p. 53, p. 56 note 80. Another, earlier, example is the disingenuous study of *S/Z* by Claude Bremond and Thomas Pavel, *De Barthes à Balzac. Fictions d'un critique, critiques d'une fiction* (Paris: Albin Michel, 1998), especially pp. 71–2.

Barthes's 'tics de langage', especially the use of 'précisément', which, we are told, Barthes deployed 'd'une manière tout à fait incongrue'.[26] Pommier cites the following important suggestion in *L'Empire des signes* by way of support for his argument:

> [L]'écriture est précisément cet acte qui unit dans le même travail ce qui ne pourrait être saisi ensemble dans le seul espace plat de la représentation.
>
> [Writing is precisely that act which unites in the same labour what could not be apprehended together in the mere flat space of representation.][27]

One critic has recently set out the varying critiques and endorsements of Barthes essay on Japan, but the disingenuous nature of Pommier's critique is astounding.[28] Pommier reminds us that Barthes makes this comment about writing whilst he is writing about 'la soupe claire' eaten daily in Japan. What detains Pommier is that he really does not understand how Barthes arrives at writing via soup. In an extraordinary gap in an understanding of the French essayistic tradition (from Montaigne to Gide), Pommier does not want to entertain – grasp, we might add – what *L'Empire des signes* is doing. Nor does he (want to) see that Barthes's Japan might be 'l'envers utopique' of *Mythologies* as one critic at the time suggested.[29] Pommier's aim by contrast is to insist that the petit bourgeois ideology of 'not seeing' (once excoriated by Barthes in his mythology 'Critique muette et aveugle') now comes back to bite the posthumous Barthes. If it is essayism that Pommier overlooks, it is also at the expense of a subtlety in Barthes's writing. For, the double grasp here, a 'stéréographie' even, is a practice that will be deconstructed across the

26   Pommier, *Grotesque de notre temps*, p. 153, p. 183 note 15.

27   Roland Barthes, *L'Empire des signes* (Geneva: Skira, 1970), henceforth referenced as ES, followed by the English version E in brackets, trans. by Richard Howard (New York: Hill & Wang, 1982); ES 25 (E 14).

28   Pamela A. Genova, 'Beyond Orientalism? Roland Barthes' Imagistic Structures of Japan', in *Romance Studies*, vol. 34, n°3–4 (2016), pp. 152–62; see also Charles Forsdick, *Travel in Twentieth-Century French and Francophone Cultures* (Oxford: Oxford University Press, 2005), pp. 137–40.

29   Jacques Ehrmann, 'L'emprise des signes', *Semiotica*, n°1 (1973), pp. 49–76 (p. 52).

essay *L'Empire des signes* as the strategy becomes how to undermine the
dialectic in its writing of food.

A more serious critique of Barthes's work points to the supposed ignorance and simplistic impressionism of Japan of the essayist. The danger
of mistaking literary essayism for ethnography notwithstanding, there is
also an argument for bending the stick towards what the Caribbean critic
Édouard Glissant calls an 'opacity', with respect to Japan.[30] If *L'Empire des
signes* – and *S/Z* – are both situated, in Marielle Macé's words, 'entre le
moment métalinguistique et le moment fictionnel', then this is reflected
in the creative freedom with which Barthes sat down in late 1969 to write
about Japan.[31] This, however, of course, does not give Barthes the right to
say just what he likes about Japan (as Pommier has implied). Indeed, the
window/countryside dialectic must respect 'parametrism', in which critique, following the 'pertinence' that Barthes found in André Martinet's
linguistics, must aim for an exactness with regard to the object observed.
Indeed, it was this 'paramétrisme' that he praised in Edgar Morin's 'écriture
dialectique'.[32] Here in 1965, about to leave for Japan for the first time, Barthes
underlined how Morin's writing was concerned not so much with being
dialectical rather how to write in a dialectical fashion. Though Barthes does
not name any of Morin's texts, one glance at the methodology section at
the end of Morin's influential account of his group's ethnographical work
in a Breton village in 1964, Plozevet, suggests a possibly important intertext
for *L'Empire des signes*.[33]

30 Édouard Glissant, 'Le chaos-monde, l'oral et l'écrit', in R. Ludwig (ed.), *Écrire la
    parole de nuit. La nouvelle littérature antillaise* (Paris: Gallimard, 1994), pp. 111–29
    (pp. 126–8).

31 Marielle Macé, *Le Temps de l'essai. Histoire d'un genre en France au XXe siècle*
    (Paris: Belin, 2006), p. 232.

32 Roland Barthes, 'Une écriture dialectique', *Combat*, 5 July 1965, p. 6 (*OC* II 718–9);
    on parametrism, see *OC* II 521. On Barthes's view of Morin's dialectical writing,
    see Andy Stafford, 'Roland Barthes, dialecticien? En dernière instance?', in Jean-
    Pierre Bertrand (ed.), *Roland Barthes: continuités*, pp. 221–46 (English version in
    the online journal *Barthes Studies*, n°3, November 2017).

33 Edgar Morin, *Commune en France. La métamorphose de Plozevet* (Paris: Fayard,
    1967), see especially pp. 403–4, on multi-dimensionality.

How then to respect parametrism in (on) Japan? Barthes's reply is clear: 'ce qui peut être visé […] c'est la possibilité d'une différence, d'une mutation, d'une révolution dans la propriété des systèmes symboliques' [What can be addressed, is the possibility of a difference, of a mutation of a revolution in the propriety of symbolic systems].[34] This mutation needs to be related to writing, which – as my subtitle suggests – involves an '*un*dialectic'. Not surprisingly the effects of this Hegelian formalism, of the open dialectic, non-synthesised, of 'two terms', are heavily used by Morin. But there is another writer who much earlier wrote using a 'double grasp'.

Writing as 'Dialecticising the Self'

'Ce livre est moi-même.'

– Jules Michelet

'[L]e voyage romantique était de tout autre effet
que le voyage moderne ; nous ne participons
jamais à un voyage que par les yeux.'

– Roland Barthes[35]

Within the 'undialectical' form of writing that Barthes develops in his creative criticism is the unhinging of the self in the writing process itself. As early as his postgraduate dissertation on ancient Greek theatre in 1941, he had used as his epigraph Paul Claudel's idea that 'Ce n'est pas un auteur qui parle, c'est une parole qui agit' [It is not a writer who speaks, but speech which acts], and Claudel has a presence in *L'Empire des signes* that has perhaps not been sufficiently explored.[36] However, if Barthes alludes

---

34   ES 10 (E 3–4).

35   Roland Barthes, *Michelet par lui-même* (Paris: Seuil, 1954), p. 20.

36   See Roland Barthes, 'Évocations et incantations dans la tragédie grecque' (1941), unpublished Sorbonne postgraduate dissertation (Archives Roland Barthes, BNF, NAF 28630), p. 1, quoting Claudel, *L'Oiseau noir dans le soleil levant* (Paris: Gallimard, 1929) p. 87. On Claudel in *L'Empire des signes*, see M. Apel-Muller,

to Claudel's *L'Oiseau noir dans le soleil levant*, the essayistic writing deployed in *L'Empire des signes* does not repeat the heavy style of Claudel's prose, nor, as we shall see, does Barthes endorse Claudel's notion of the Japanese soul.[37] If the Bunraku has multiple authors, the decentring of self can be seen most keenly in Barthes's early writing on Jules Michelet.[38]

In 1951, in his first publication on Michelet (and his first in *Esprit*), we find Barthes beginning to theorise a 'double grasp' used by the historian. Michelet is not only 'mangeur de l'Histoire' [eater of History] and 'nageur dans l'Histoire' [swimmer in History], but also the person who walks *with* the actors of History – 'le peuple' – whilst remaining blind, so to speak, as to the outcome of their actions. With this gymnastic form of the dialectic (at once, in temporal terms, here *and* there), Michelet is, wrote Barthes, 'voyageur puis spectateur, mangeur et puis ruminant de l'Histoire' [traveller then spectator, eater and then ruminator of History].[39] In opposition to the 'récit' [narrative] normally associated with history-writing, Michelet combines the 'tableau' with the 'survol' [flying over] allowing him to be a 'marcheur' [walker] with the people whose 'history' he is writing. Barthes suggests that this leads to a new split: 'ou bien le malaise du cheminement, ou bien l'euphorie du panorama' [either the malaise of the slow advance, or else the euphoria of the panorama]; such is the price (as it were) for Michelet of what Barthes calls '[c]ette double saisie' [this double grasp].[40] But the 'double saisie' brings other benefits to Barthes's mind. By sometimes leaving behind the History in which he is rowing ('rame'), Michelet's prose displays moments of surprise in which the historian, the 'voyageur', stops to look, and here is 'un second plan d'histoire, celle-ci toute panoramique,

---

'La Nouvelle critique a lu', *La Nouvelle Critique*, n°40 (January 1971); see also Christophe Corbier, 'Nietzsche, Brecht, Claudel: Barthes face à la tragédie musicale grecque', *Revue de littérature comparée*, vol. 353 (2015), pp. 5–28.

37   Claudel's much earlier set of essays *Connaissance de l'est* (1900) is also cited as an intertext for *L'Empire des signes* (Genova, 'Beyond Orientalism?', p. 157).

38   ES 75 (E 54–5).

39   Roland Barthes, 'Michelet, l'Histoire et la mort' (1951), *OC* I 110–2; Barthes, *Michelet*, p. 21; trans. by Richard Miller (Berkeley: University of California Press, 1987), pp. 20–2.

40   Barthes, *Michelet*, p. 20.

faite d'intellection' [a second level of history, which is completely pano-
ramic, made of intellection].[41] Against the distance of History which he
narrates and puts into forms, Michelet, suggests Barthes in 1951, could use
an innovation of writing, which will resurface in Barthes's own writing on
Japan: namely, a dialectical form:

> L'altérité des objets historiques [dans Michelet] n'est jamais totale, l'Histoire
> est toujours familière, car le Temps n'est là que pour soutenir une identité ; son
> mouvement est équationnel, sa dialectique à deux termes.

> [The alterity of historical objects is never total, History is always familiar, because
> Time is there only to sustain an identity; History's movement is equational, its dia-
> lectic of two terms.][42]

We saw this two-term dialectic in the designation of Racine's world as
unmediated and intransitive; and it is precisely this dialectic that now we
trace and then explore in *L'Empire des signes*; to suggest that it is almost
as if, by visiting what we might call an epistemological Japan, Barthes
was setting about renewing Michelet's 'double grasp', renewing its use
100 years after its first deployment.

One of the clearest examples of the experimental practice of dialectical
writing in Barthes's case are in his diaries written during his 1974 visit to
China – the country of the Maoist dialectic – but whose publication was
abandoned by Barthes and published only posthumously.[43] Despite the
scepticism that we saw above to the ability to write dialectically, Barthes
nevertheless tried to do so in the *Carnets du voyage en Chine*. Not published in his lifetime, these writings, we must assume, were considered a
failure (but thereby giving the *Carnets de Chine* a feel of experimentation).[44]

---

41   *Ibid.*, p. 22.
42   Barthes, 'Michelet, l'Histoire et la Mort', *OC* I 111 (my translation).
43   Barthes, *Carnets de Chine*, pp. 78–9, p. 206; see Andy Stafford, 'Roland Barthes's
      Travels in China: Writing a Diary of Dissidence within Dissidence?', *Textual
      Practice*, vol. 30, n°2 (2016), special number 'Deliberations: The Journals of Roland
      Barthes', ed. by Neil Badmington, pp. 287–304 (republished by Routledge in
      May 2017).
44   *Incidents* written in and on Morocco, just after he wrote *L'Empire des signes* in 1969,
      is another example of Barthes's travel writing that remained unpublished in his
      lifetime.

Therefore, with Barthes's writings on China and Morocco never given his imprimatur, *L'Empire des signes* must, as the only published 'récit de voyage', be considered successful. Furthermore, *L'Empire des signes* seems to enjoy a freedom from political pressures. Whereas China gives energy to French Maoism at the beginning of the 1970s – and even *Mythologies*, as an ethnography of France in the 1950s, showed a political engagement – Japan for Barthes did not require any external dialectic: there is no 'Alors, le Japon?' to write on his return.

Indeed, if the '*in*dialectique' becomes a way of attacking the totalitarian 'brique' of Maoist China, it has a different function in Japan. *Un*dialectics becomes a starting point for an essayistic and 'romanesque' form of writing that begins to unhinge the Western self: Japan 'l'a mis en situation d'écriture': 'Cette situation [...] opère un certain ébranlement de la personne, un renversement des anciennes lectures, une secousse du sens, déchiré, exténué' [This situation of writing is the very one in which a certain disturbance of the person occurs, a subversion of earlier readings, a shock of meaning, lacerated, extenuated].[45] This does not preclude a political reading of *L'Empire des signes*, but it may involve asking different questions than on China. If Western, Hegelian dialectics is too methodical for Japan, then in the double grasp of semiology, will the signifier simply be privileged over the signified? Does an ascetic sumptuousness allow the hand to move the pen – to the extent that Diana Knight has suggested a sexual analogy of masturbation with pachinko?[46] It is in the deployment and the undermining of the double grasp that this political reading will emerge.

In order to trace the dialectical – or rather undialectical – strategies in *L'Empire des signes* we must start with Barthes's view on Japanese grammar that he had given in 1968:

> le japonais fait du sujet, non l'agent tout-puissant du discours, mais plutôt un grand espace obstiné qui enveloppe l'énoncé et se déplace avec lui.

---

45 ES 11 (E 4).
46 Diana Knight, *Barthes and Utopia. Space, Travel, Writing* (Oxford: Clarendon Press, 1997), p. 164.

[Japanese makes the subject not into the all-powerful agent of discourse but rather into a great, stubborn space enveloping the statement and moving about with it][47]

Is this similar to the 'se dialectiser' that we saw above? It does indeed suggest that, firstly, Barthes is looking for a parametric form of writing and, secondly, this discourse uses a 'double grasp', even a 'dialectic of two terms'. In this way, the 'double grasp' that Barthes discovered in historiography of a distant past in Michelet's historiography starts to mutate. Moreover, in his 1941 post-graduate thesis, Barthes had brought together ancient Greek theatre, armed with its spoken and performed dialectic, with the Japan in Paul Claudel's work. Here in 1970 by contrast, there is nothing of the sort. In *L'Empire des signes*, Barthes goes beyond many aspects of dialectics that are implicit in notions of intersubjectivity – be it of a Sartre or of a Merleau-Ponty.

Thus, the human subject speaking in Japanese, 'cette grande enveloppe vide de la parole', is decentred. Indeed, this implicit discussion with Sartre's and phenomenology in *L'Etre et le néant*, and its phenomenological insistence that consciousness is consciousness of something, is precisely that which the Japanese verb seems, to Barthes, to undermine:

> comment pouvons-nous imaginer un verbe qui soit à la fois sans sujet, sans attribut, et cependant transitif, comme par exemple un acte de connaissance sans sujet connaissant et sans objet connu?

> [how can we *imagine* a verb which is simultaneously without subject, without attribute, and yet transitive, such as for instance an act of knowledge without knowing subject and without known object?][48]

What Barthes calls (with a glance towards Japanese martial arts) 'ces exercices d'une grammaire aberrante', then opens out onto a political discourse in *L'Empire des signes*, by deploying a truncated dialectic: Japanese, Japan, as an empty critique of the West, 'de l'idéologie même de notre parole' [the very ideology of our speech].[49] *Pace* René Pommier, this

---

47   Roland Barthes, 'Drame, poème, roman', *OC* V 587 note II; trans. by Philip Thody, *Writer Sollers* (Minneapolis: University of Minnesota Press, 1987), p. 45 (translation modified).

48   ES 16 (E 7).

49   ES 17 (E 8).

politicised essayism that alights on Japanese food as a meal that is 'décentré' is a deliberate ploy: it allows Barthes to forestall, truncate (rather than refuse) the dialectical. Rather than an orientalist tract or a penetrating view of Japan, his essay declines to comment, except to construct Japan as the paradoxa to the West, like a Japanese present he brings back to Europe but which is an empty box. It is an undialectical synthesis of the double grasp that seems to allow this 'mutation' [shift].

Thus, the 'double grasp' of a Michelet seems to move, in Barthes's writing of the Japanese meal, towards a critique of the very notion of 'saisie'. Firstly, the danger of a positivism is refused by Barthes. This refusal uses an appropriately 'abyssal' style, what he called the writing 'd'abîme en abîme' used by Nietzsche.[50] It is evident in the following list:

> un vide de parole […] constitue l'écriture ; […] le Zen, dans l'exemption de tout sens, écrit les jardins, les gestes, les maisons, les bouquets, les visages, la violence.
>
> Le rêve : connaître une langue étrangère (étrange) et cependant ne pas la comprendre […].
>
> [an emptiness of language constitutes writing; Zen, in the exemption from all meaning, writes gardens, gestures, houses, flower arrangements, faces, violence. / The dream: to know a foreign (alien) language and yet not to understand it.][51]

The jolt that generates this abyssal way of writing is provided by the word 'violence', following as it does a list of pastoral thematics. The jolt is repeated in another abrupt ending in 'Sans adresse', in which Barthes moves seamlessly from the level of culture to that of writing: 'visiter un lieu pour la première fois, c'est de la sorte commencer à l'écrire; l'adresse n'étant pas écrite, il faut bien qu'elle fonde elle-même sa propre écriture' [to visit a place for the first time is thereby to begin to write it: the address not being written, it must establish its own writing].[52] If there is a 'double grasp' in these early examples, as we go through the essay the very notion of grasp begins, especially in the second half of *L'Empire des signes*, to melt away.

---

50   On Nietzsche's 'abyssal' style, see Barthes, *The Grain of the Voice*, p. 72.
51   ES 12–3 (E 4–6).
52   ES 51 (E 36).

'Aucun vouloir-saisir' versus 'la double saisie' ?

Barthes begins his description flattering our perception, based on our reading of the tableau – and let us not forget that, for Barthes, it is the combination of the 'tableau' and the 'survol' in Michelet's writing which is the basis of the 'double grasp'. Citing Piero della Francesca, Barthes designates our 'double grasp' reading method as alternating between surfaces and bodies; but it is an essayistic trap: we must read the tray of Japanese dishes in a radically different way, Barthes insinuates:

> un tel ordre, délicieux lorsqu'il apparaît, est destiné à être défait, refait selon le rythme même de l'alimentation ; ce qui était tableau figé au départ, devient établi ou échiquier, espace, non d'une vue, mais d'un faire ou d'un jeu.
>
> [such an order, delicious when it appears, is destined to be undone, recomposed according to the very rhythm of eating; what was motionless tableau at the start becomes a work-bench or chessboard, the space not of seeing but of doing – of *praxis* or play][53]

This game – or 'work' – marks the way food is eaten in Japan:

> [cette] sorte de travail ou de jeu […] porte moins sur la transformation de la matière première ([…] la cuisine japonaise est peu cuisinée […]) que sur l'assemblage mouvant et comme inspiré d'éléments dont l'ordre de prélèvement n'est fixé par aucun protocole : […] vous faites vous-même ce que vous mangez ; le mets n'est plus un produit réifié, dont la préparation est, chez nous, pudiquement éloignée […].
>
> [this kind of work or play bears less on the transformation of the primary substance (Japanese food is rarely cooked) than on the shifting and somehow inspired assemblage of elements whose order of selection is fixed by no protocol: you yourself make what it is you eat; the dish is no longer a reified product, whose preparation is, among us, modestly distanced in time and space][54]

In opposition to the passivity of the person eating a Western dish, Barthes is struck by the activity before the Japanese dish; and this activity seems to replace the Western gaze (both penetrating and surface) – and maybe

53   ES 21 (E 11).
54   ES 22 (E 12).

already the 'double grasp' – which is our only activity: whereas *over there* he notices, on the part of the person eating, a direct agency (i.e. unmediated) *on* what they are eating.

There is undoubtedly a very classical, dialectical formation here; however, Barthes, ever the drifter, is very quick to undo the dialectic by truncating it; in the same way as he begins to consider the clothing item from 1967 onwards, here writing on Japan, he undermines the power of determination by inverting it. The two examples he uses are the smallness of food in Japan and then the function of chopsticks:

> Il y a convergence du minuscule et du comestible : les choses ne sont petites que pour être mangées mais aussi, elles sont comestibles pour accomplir leur essence, qui est la petitesse. L'accord de la nourriture orientale et de la baguette ne peut être seulement fonctionnel, instrumental ; les aliments sont coupés pour pouvoir être saisis par la baguette, mais aussi la baguette existe parce que les aliments sont coupés en petits morceaux ; un même mouvement, une même forme transcende la matière et son outil : la division.

> [There is a convergence of the tiny and the esculent: things are not only small in order to be eaten, but are also comestible in order to fulfil their essence, which is smallness. The harmony between Oriental food and chopsticks cannot be merely functional, instrumental; the foodstuffs are cut up so they can be grasped by the sticks, but also the chopsticks exist because the foodstuffs are cut into small pieces; one and the same movement, one and the same form transcends the substance and its utensil: division.][55]

If there is a sort of 'double grasp' here, it is operated as an equalisation, or levelling, of former hierarchies; Hegel has not so much seen his dialectic turned on its head rather denied its dialectical synthesis: it has been reversed and turned inside out.

This levelling of determinants – this overturning of Hegel, we might say – returns in the chopstick – which is 'la double baguette' as Barthes calls it.[56] The material act of eating by bringing food to the mouth using chopsticks belongs also to another function, namely the 'déictique' (or semiological) act of pointing to the food; this fine, almost delicate, act is

55   ES 26–7 (E 15–6).
56   ES 27 (E 16).

thus compared to that involved in the West of eating using a knife and fork. Deploying a wide functionalism, Barthes equalises – if not overthrows – the determining order in the act of eating: the chopsticks show, point to, what they are going to put in the mouth. There is a sort of finesse which complements the suppleness of the dialectic with which Barthes represents the Japanese act of eating in a sort of multi-tasking. And it is what leads him – in an essayistic fashion – to distinguish two types of agency: 'l'oiseau' (in a reference to Claudel) of the chopsticks – which pinches the food – versus the Western 'prédateur' of the fork which pierces it.

The expert writer of the provisional/peremptory (in the neat, double expression proposed by Marielle Macé), the Nietzschean writer who writes 'd'abîme en abîme', has other strategies for undermining continuous prose: that is, by using essayistic writing in one long sentence. 'La crudité' is made up entirely of two sentences only; the first is ten lines long, the second, thirty-two: Proust – even Philippe Sollers – would have been proud of this 'uninterrupted text' indeed.[57] The essayistic flow – working in an opposing fashion to the 'abyssal' style discussed above – is clear to see here; but it is the last line of this section which matters for our analysis of the 'indialectique', in which the analysis moves to another level. From this section of *L'Empire des signes* onwards, writing and object begin to become conflated in 'la pincée d'écriture'.[58] Furthermore, what Barthes calls 'l'illusion de totalité' – linked to his critique of the Western 'âme', especially in Claudel's conception – is radically contrasted, by the work of communication in Japan in which there lurks an agency which is not interiorised:

> Dans le *Bunraku* […], la marionnette ne singeant plus la créature, l'homme n'est plus une marionnette entre les mains de la divinité, le dedans ne commande plus le dehors.
>
> [In *Bunraku*, since the puppet no longer apes the creature, man is no longer a puppet in the divinity's hands, the inside no longer commands the outside][59]

57   ES 33–4 (E 20–1).
58   ES 75 (E 55, 'sliver of writing' in the English translation misses the allusion in 'pincée' to the chopsticks' way of picking up food).
59   ES 84 (E 62).

Not only does the exteriority represent a refusal of depth, of the hidden, of the intimate, Barthes hints that the Bunraku puppet involves a human activity that is non-passive and which undermines the Western 'person'; and the critique of Western personalism is continued in the critique of intersubjectivity implied in the 'qui salue qui ?' caption.[60] Indeed, in Japan, communication itself is thwarted by a spiritual emptying of self:

> Tout le Zen [...] apparaît ainsi comme une immense pratique destinée à arrêter le langage, à casser cette sorte de radiophonie intérieure qui émet continûment en nous.

> [All of Zen thus appears as an enormous praxis destined to halt language, to jam that kind of internal radiophony continually sending in us][61]

The Haiku is deemed to be one that has a 'justesse' that is parametric, as Barthes puts it in a parenthesis:

> (qui n'est nullement peinture exacte du réel, mais adéquation du signifiant et du signifié, suppression des marges, bavures et interstices qui d'ordinaire excèdent ou ajourent le rapport sémantique)

> [which is not at all an exact depiction of reality, but an adequation of signifier and signified, a suppression of margins, smudges, and interstices which usually exceed or perforate the semantic relation][62]

Japan shows a 'dialectique nouvelle' in *L'Empire des signes*, and we will not be surprised to see that – given that the writer dialecticised themselves in the quotation above – the new dialectic touches the person. In opposition to the arrogant notion of the human soul in Western romanticism – a soul that Claudel designates as centrally Japanese – Barthes proposes a Japanese route towards a true liberation of the self, undermining the coded self in the West, towards a free form of personality in which we quote but never incarnate (hence the surprising clothing combinations he notices in Japan).[63] In an ironic, dialectical way, this new person

---

60   ES 85, 87, 89 (E 64–5, 68).
61   ES 99 (E 74).
62   ES 101 (E 75–6). On parametric 'justesse' see Barthes, *Critique et vérité* (1965) *OC* II 797.
63   ES 131–2 (E 97).

derives from quantity (the millions of bodies in Japan); and it arrives also in a deeply Hegelian voice:

> On dirait que le Japon impose la même dialectique à ses corps qu'à ses objets : voyez le rayon des mouchoirs dans un grand magasin : innombrables, tous dissemblables et cependant nulle intolérance à la série, nulle subversion de l'ordre. Ou encore le haïku : combien de haïku dans l'histoire du Japon ? [...] Le résultat – ou l'enjeu – de cette dialectique est le suivant : le corps japonais va jusqu'au bout de son individualité [...] : elle est pure de toute hystérie, ne vise pas à faire de l'individu un corps original, distingué des autres corps [...]. L'individualité [...] est simplement différence, réfractée, sans privilège, de corps en corps.

> [One might say Japan imposes the same dialectic on its bodies as on its objects: look at the handkerchief shelf in a department store: countless, all different, yet no intolerance in the series, no subversion of order. Or again, the haiku: how many haiku in the history of Japan? The result – or the stake – of this dialectic is the following: the Japanese body achieves the limit of its individuality: it is pure of all hysteria, does not aim at making the individual into an original body, distinguished from other bodies. Individuality is simply difference, refracted, without privilege, from body to body][64]

'Sans privilège': the equalisation – the 'dialectic of two terms', we might say – is in full flow, going towards the void, by deploying the abyss, *both* in the 'countryside' *and* in the 'window'.[65] Indeed, the reversibility of determinants, the equalisation of differences, the tactical *de*-hierarchisation, opens out onto, works towards, the void: 'Aucun vouloir-saisir et cependant aucune oblation' [no will-to-seize and yet no offering up] is

---

64   ES 132–3 (E 97–8).
65   A good example is the jump between pages 138 and 139 (E 102–3); following a fine excursus on the eye-lid, Barthes moves abruptly to the Zengakuren, in 'L'écriture de la violence' (albeit cleverly prepared by the vigorous playing of Pachinko in a much earlier section, ES 42 / E 28). Furthermore, the description of the militant political action overturns the expected determinants: the Zengakuren shout slogans that are 'vides', phatic even – 'Les zengakuren vont se battre' – as a way of mobilising. Is this politicised form of phatic language an example of what Barthes meant in his 'wood-cutter' response to Marx's cherry-tree mentioned above, in that the Zengakuren slogan is a *direct* political language act? In designating 'cette action elle-même' as 'pure', Barthes's argument contrasts sharply with John Berger's Sorelian 'symbolism' in his 1968 essay 'The Nature of Mass Demonstrations', see John Berger, *Selected Writings* (London: Bloomsbury, 2001), pp. 246–9.

the penultimate caption next to an anodyne photograph of a domestic room.[66] The 'double grasp' has indeed mutated, if not been abolished, and if we think back to the impasse of the window/countryside, it might even have been resolved.

Conclusion: Undialectics and Haiku

As Michelet did with history ('refaire la vie des morts') – bringing the *there* of the past to the *now* of the historian's writing – Barthes does for the same for Japan 'là-bas'; in other words, the isomorphism Michelet/ History with Barthes/Japan – the past, as we say in English after all, is a foreign country – suggests a distance that must be addressed by a 'double grasp'. But we are also living in a post-68 world, and 1969 is often cited as a hellish realisation of the failure of May 1968 to overthrow the system. 'Vivre dans l'inhabitable' in 1970 might not entail for Barthes a search for nihilism – or if it does, it is a productive, pleasurable nihilism. Indeed, the poet Georges Perros, on finishing reading *L'Empire des signes*, wanted Barthes to 'japoniser le monde entier' [japanise the whole world].[67]

The undialectical – the critique of Hegelian dialectics – that we have seen in Barthes's double grasp leads to a provisional if predictable suggestion: that the Haiku *is* undialectics. But in what way could the paradoxical, the suspension or the dialectic, the forestalling of synthesis be deeply linked to the haiku? We can certainly see an 'antithetical', if not paradoxical, form in Barthesian writing.[68] In *L'Empire des signes*, it is ultimately the 'Western' dialectic that Barthes deconstructs, so as to found a new one – explicitly in the section 'des millions de corps' onwards – ; but this dialectic is one which is, or, leads to, the void, or rather which leads only to the void. This

---

66   ES 149 (the caption and photograph are both, inexplicably, excluded from the English version).

67   Georges Perros, *Papiers collés vol. II* (Paris: Gallimard, 1973), p. 295.

68   On this, see Charles Coustille, *Antithèses. Mallarmé, Céline, Péguy, Paulhan, Barthes* (Paris: Gallimard, 2018).

is a dialectic of two terms – truncated, amputated, 'open', but thereby modernised, globalised, intensified: a hyper-dialectic. And finally, the undialectic is that which lives a double life, that is, within writing itself; in writing, it is the dialectic of the abyss, the deployment of the peremptory/ provisional as undialectical writing (as opposed to its negative-dialectical counterpart), but which is alternated – just as in Nietzsche – with the writing of flow. The undialectical is the overcoming of determinisms: the outside has won out over the inside; in short, a new writing. This seems to be intricately linked to the haiku. Consider the way one Japanese critic, Seki Osuga Otsuji, described the haiku and its grasp:

> If one does not grasp something – something which does not merely touch us through our senses but contacts the life within and has the dynamic form of nature – no matter how cunningly we form our words, they will give only a hollow sound. Those who compose haiku without grasping anything are merely exercising their ingenuity. The ingenious become only selectors of words and cannot create new experiences from themselves.[69]

In the haiku, in the undialectical, 'Il n'y a rien à *saisir*' [there is nothing to *grasp*]; in a move that foresees the 'neutral' in his work, Barthes questions grasp fundamentally, developing what he will later call the 'NVS' – the 'non-vouloir-saisir' [no-wish-to-grasp]. This is not only a reversal in re-spect of Michelet's 'double grasp'; it may also be the effect of the essay in critical mode, a creative criticism, even an essayistic poetry – what Barthes called a 'disalienation': an *écriture* which, in our troubled world, we might want to consider as one of life's pleasures.[70]

69 Seki Osuga Otsuji, *Otsuji Hairon-shû* (1947), cited in Kenneth Yasuda, *The Japanese Haiku* (Rutland, VT; Tokyo: Charles E. Tuttle Company, 1957), p. 29.
70 Interview with Barthes in the *Tribune de Genève*, 15 April 1970, *OC* III 654.

Bibliography

Alter, Robert, *The Pleasures of Reading in an Ideological Age* (New York: Simon & Schuster, 1989).

Aristotle, *On the Art of Poetry*, trans. by T. S. Dorsch, in *Classical Literary Criticism* (Middlesex: Penguin Books, 1965), pp. 29–75.

Ayres, Philip J., 'Marston's *Antonio's Revenge*: The Morality of the Revenging Hero', *Studies in English Literature, 1500–1900*, vol. 12, n°2 (1972), pp. 359–74.

Bakhtin, Mikhail, *Problems of Dostoevsky's Poetics*, ed. and trans. by Caryl Emerson (Minneapolis: University of Minnesota Press, 1984).

Baldick, Chris (ed.), *The Oxford Dictionary of Literary Terms*, 3rd edn (Oxford: Oxford University Press, 2008).

Barthes, Roland, *Camera Lucida: Reflections on Photography* (1980), trans. by Richard Howard (New York: Hill and Wang, 1981).

——, *Empire of Signs* (1970), trans. by Richard Howard (New York: Hill and Wang, 1983).

——, 'From Work to Text', in *The Rustle of Language*, trans. by Richard Howard (New York: Hill and Wang, 1986), pp. 56–64.

——, *Image-Music-Text*, trans. by Stephen Heath (New York: Hill and Wang, 1978).

——, *Mythologies: The Complete Edition, in a New Translation*, trans. by Richard Howard and Annette Lavers (New York: Hill and Wang, 2013).

——, *The Pleasure of the Text* (1970), trans. by Richard Miller (New York: Hill and Wang, 1975).

——, *The Preparation of the Novel: Lecture Courses and Seminars at the Collège de France, 1978–1979 and 1979–1980*, trans. by Kate Briggs (New York: Columbia University Press, 2010).

——, *S/Z: An Essay* (1970), trans. by Richard Miller (New York: Hill and Wang, 1974).

——, *Writing Degree Zero* (1953), trans. by Annette Lavers and Colin Smith (New York: Hill and Wang, 1977).

Benstock, Sari, 'At the Margin of Discourse: Footnotes in the Fictional Text', *PMLA*, vol. 98, n°2 (1983), pp. 204–25.

Bergson, Allen, 'Dramatic Style as Parody in Marston's Antonio and Mellida', *Studies in English Literature, 1500–1900*, vol. 11, n°2 (1971), pp. 307–25.

Bergson, Henri, 'Laughter', in *Comedy: 'An Essay on Comedy' by George Meredith, 'Laughter' by Henri Bergson*, ed. by Wylie Sypher (Baltimore, MD: John Hopkins University Press, 1980), pp. 61–190.

Bersani, Leo, *Freudian Body: Psychoanalysis and Art* (New York: Columbia University Press, 1986).

Blake, Ann, '"The Humour of Children": John Marston's Plays in the Private Theatres', *Review of English Studies*, New Series, vol. 38, n°152 (1987), pp. 471–82.

Bowersock, Glen W., 'The Art of the Footnote', *The American Scholar*, vol. 53, n°1 (1984), pp. 54–62.

Brooke, Nicholas, *Horrid Laughter in Jacobean Tragedy* (London: Open Books, 1979).

Bruster, Douglas, and Robert Weimann, *Prologues to Shakespeare's Theatre: Performance and Liminality in Early Modern Drama* (London: Routledge, 2004).

Butler, Christopher, *Pleasure and the Arts: Enjoying Literature, Painting, and Music* (Oxford: Oxford University Press, 2005).

Cooper, Sarah, *The Soul of Film Theory* (London: Palgrave Macmillan, 2013).

Crary, Jonathan, *Techniques of the Observer. On Vision and Modernity in the Nineteenth Century* (Cambridge, MA: MIT Press, 1992).De Man, Paul, 'Pascal's Allegory of Persuasion', in *Aesthetic Ideology*, ed. by Andrzej Warminski (Minneapolis: University of Minnesota Press, 1996), pp. 51–69.

De Quincey, Thomas, *The Collected Works of Thomas De Quincey. Volume X: Literary Theory and Criticism*, ed. by David Masson (Edinburgh: Black, 1990).

Deleuze, Gilles, *Cinema 1: The Movement-Image*, trans. by Hugh Tomlinson and Barbara Habberjam (London: Athlone, 1986).

Derrida, Jacques, 'Les Morts de Roland Barthes', *Poétique*, n°47 (1981), pp. 269–92.

Dollimore, Jonathan, and Alan Sinfield, 'History and Ideology: The Instance of *Henry V*', in *Alternative Shakespeares*, ed. by John Drakakis (London: Methuen, 1985), pp. 206–27.

Dunne, Derek, '"Partialitie in a Judge, is a Turpitude": Partial Judges and Judicious Revengers in Early Modern English Drama', in *The Emergence of Impartiality: Towards a History of Objectivity*, ed. by Kathryn Murphy and Anita Traninger (Leiden: Brill, 2013), pp. 171–88.

Ebert, Teresa, and Mas'ud Zavarzadeh, *Class in Culture* (Boulder, CO: Paradigm, 2008).

Eco, Umberto, *The Role of the Reader: Explorations in the Semiotics of Texts* (Bloomington: Indiana University Press, 1984).

Empson, William, *The Structure of Complex Words* (New York: New Directions, 1951).

Felman, Shoshana, 'Postal Survival, or The Question of the Navel', *Yale French Studies*, n°69 (1985), pp. 49–72.

Flieger, Jerry Aline, *The Purloined Punch Line: Freud's Comic Theory and the Postmodern Text* (Baltimore, MD: The John Hopkins University Press, 1991).

Foakes, Reginald A., 'John Marston's Fantastical Plays: *Antonio and Mellida* and *Antonio's Revenge*', *Philological Quarterly*, vol. 41, n°1 (1962), pp. 229–39.

——, 'Tragicomedy and Comic Form', in *Comedy from Shakespeare to Sheridan: Change and Continuity in the English and European Dramatic Tradition*, ed. by A. R. Braunmuller and J. C. Bulman (Newark: University of Delaware Press, 1986), pp. 74–88.

Ford, John, *'Tis Pity She's a Whore*, ed. by Martin Wiggins (London: Bloomsbury, 2003).

Forest, Philippe, *Haiku, etc. Allaphbed 4* (Nantes: Cécile Defaut, 2008).

——, *La Beauté du contresens et autres essais sur la littérature japonaise* (Nantes: Cécile Défaut, 2005).

Forsdick, Charles, '"(In)connaissance de l'Asie": Barthes and Bouvier, China and Japan', *Modern & Contemporary France*, vol. 14, n°1 (2006), pp. 63–77.

Foucault, Michel, *The Order of Things: An Archaeology of the Human Sciences* (1966), trans. by Alan Sheridan (New York and London: Routledge, 2002).

——, 'What Is an Author?', *Modern Criticism and Theory: A Reader*, ed. by David Lodge (London: Longman, 1988), pp. 197–210.

Freud, Sigmund, 'Beyond the Pleasure Principle', in *The Standard Edition of the Complete Psychological Works of Sigmund Freud*, vol. XVIII (London: Hogarth, 1955), pp. 1–64.

Frye, Northrop, *Anatomy of Criticism: Four Essays* (Princeton, NJ: Princeton University Press, 1957).

Genette, Gérard, *Palimpsests: Literature in the Second Degree*, trans. by Channa Newman and Claude Doubinsky (Lincoln: University of Nebraska Press, 1997).

——, *Paratexts: Thresholds of Interpretation*, trans. by Jane E. Lewin (Cambridge: Cambridge University Press, 2001).

Genova, Pamela A., 'Beyond Orientalism? Roland Barthes' Imagistic Structures of Japan', in *Romance Studies*, vol. 34, n°3–4 (2016), pp. 152–62.

Goffman, Erving, *Interaction Ritual. Essays on Face-to-Face Behaviour* (London: Penguin Books, 1967).

——, *The Presentation of Self in Everyday Life* (London: Penguin Books, 1959).

Guarini, Giambattista, *Compendio della Poesia Tragicomica*, trans. by Damiano Pietropaulo, in *Sources of Dramatic Theory*, ed. by Michael J. Sidnall (Cambridge: Cambridge University Press, 1991).

Hegel, Georg Wilhelm Friedrich, *Aesthetics. Lectures on Fine Art*, vol. 1, trans. by Thomas Malcom Knox (Oxford: Clarendon Press, 1975).

Hitchens, Christopher, *The Monarchy: A Critique of Britain's Favorite Fetish* (London: Vintage Digital, 2012).

Howell, Brian, 'Chris Marker's Real and Unreal Japan – *Sans Soleil* as Intercultural Document', *Language, Culture, and Communication*, vol. 9 (2017), pp. 149–59.

Hutcheon, Linda, *A Theory of Parody: The Teachings of Twentieth-Century Art Forms* (New York: Methuen, 1985).

Iversen, Margaret, *Beyond Pleasure: Freud, Lacan, Barthes* (Philadelphia: Pennsylvania State University Press, 2007).

Jacobs, Alan, *The Pleasures of Reading in an Age of Distraction* (New York: Oxford University Press, 2011).

Jensen, Ejner J., 'The Style of the Boy Actors', *Comparative Drama*, vol. 2, n°2 (1968), pp. 100–14.

Johnson, Samuel, 'Of Textual Notes', 'Preface to Shakespeare', in *The Yale Edition of the Works of Samuel Johnson*, ed. by Arthur Sherbo (New York: Yale University Press, 1968), vol. 7, pp. 59–113.

——, 'The Plays of William Shakespeare', in *The Major Works*, ed. by Donald Greene (Oxford: Oxford University Press, 1984), pp. 419–66.

Kant, Immanuel, *Critique of Judgement*, trans. by James Creed Meredith, ed. by Nicholas Walker (Oxford: Oxford University Press, 2007).

Karatani, Kojin, *History and Repetition*, ed. by Seiji M. Lippit (New York: Columbia University Press, 2003).

——, 'Uses of Aesthetics: After Orientalism', *Boundary Two*, vol. 25, n°2 (1998), pp. 145–60.

Kirby, John T., 'Aristotle on Metaphor', *The American Journal of Philology*, vol. 118, n°4 (1997), pp. 517–54.

Knight, Diana, *Barthes and Utopia: Space, Travel, Writing* (Oxford: Clarendon, 1997).

Kosik, Karel, *La Dialectique du concret*, trans. from the German by Roger Dangeville (Paris: Maspero, 1970).

Kyd, Thomas, *The Spanish Tragedy*, ed. by David Bevington (Manchester: Manchester University Press, 1996).

Leech, Clifford, *Tragedy* (London: Routledge, 1969).

Lewis, Paul, *Comic Effects: Interdisciplinary Approaches to Humor in Literature* (Albany: State University of New York Press, 1989).

Lupton, Catherine, *Chris Marker: Memories of the Future* (London: Reaktion Books, 2005).

MacCabe, Colin, 'Barthes and Bazin: The Ontology of the Image', in *Writing the Image after Roland Barthes*, ed. by Jean-Michel Rabaté (Philadelphia, PA: University of Pennsylvania Press, 1997), pp. 71–6.

Marker, Chris, *Le Dépays* (Paris: Herscher, 1982).

Marston, John, *Antonio and Mellida: The First Part*, ed. by G. K. Hunter (London: Edward Arnold, 1965).

——, *Antonio's Revenge*, ed. by Reavley Gair (Manchester: Manchester University Press, 1978).

——, *The Malcontent*, ed. by W. David Kay (London: A&C Black, 1998).

McGrath, Thomas, *New and Selected Poems* (Ohio: Swallow Press, 1964).

Mehlman, Jeffrey, *Revolution and Repetition: Marx/Hugo/Balzac* (Berkeley: University of California Press, 1977).

Möller, Olaf, 'Chris Marker: Ghost World. Japan Through the Looking Glass', *Film Comment* (July/August 2003), pp. 35–7.

Phillips, Adam, *On Kissing, Tickling, and Being Bored: Psychoanalytic Essays on the Unexamined Life* (Cambridge: Harvard University Press, 1993).

Pinguet, Maurice, *Le Texte Japon, introuvables et inédits*, ed. by Michaël Ferrier (Paris: Seuil, 2009).

Rose, Margaret, *Parody: Ancient, Modern, and Post-Modern* (Cambridge: Cambridge University Press, 1993).

Saito, Yuriko, *Everyday Aesthetics* (Oxford: Oxford University Press, 2010).

——, *Aesthetics of the Familiar: Everyday Life and World-Making* (Oxford: Oxford University Press, 2017).

Schoenbaum, Samuel, 'The Precarious Balance of John Marston', *PMLA*, vol. 67, n°7 (1952), pp. 1069–78.

Segalen, Victor, *Essai sur l'exotisme* (Paris: Le Livre de Poche, 1999).

Shakespeare, William, *Hamlet*, ed. by G. R. Hibbard (Oxford: Oxford University Press, 1987).

——, *Henry V*, ed. by Gary Taylor, in *William Shakespeare, The Complete Works*, 2nd edn (Oxford: Oxford University Press, 2005), pp. 595–625.

Sheringham, Michael, *Everyday Life: Theories and Practices from Surrealism to the Present* (Oxford: Oxford University Press, 2006).

Shklovsky, Viktor, 'Art as Technique', trans. by Lee T. Lemon and Marion J. Reis, in *Modern Criticism and Theory: A Reader,* ed. by David Lodge (London: Longmans, 1988), pp. 16–30.

Simmel, Georg, 'The Metropolis and Mental Life' (1903), in *The Blackwell City Reader*, ed. by Gary Bridge and Sophie Watson (Oxford and Malden, MA: Wiley-Blackwell, 2002).

Sontag, Susan, 'Writing Itself: On Roland Barthes', in *A Barthes Reader*, ed. by Susan Sontag (New York: Hill and Wang, 1982).

Steiner, George, *The Death of Tragedy* (New Haven, CT: Yale University Press, 1996).

Stendhal [*né* Marie-Henri Beyle], *Mémoires d'un touriste* (Paris: Le Divan, 1929).

——, *The Red and the Black*, trans. by Catherine Slater (Oxford: Oxford University Press, 1991).

Trifonas, Peter Pericles, *Barthes and the Empire of Signs* (Cambridge: Icon Books, 2001).

Ungar, Steven, 'Persistence of the Image: Barthes, Photography and the Resistance to Film', in *Critical Essays on Roland Barthes*, ed. by Diana Knight (New York: Hamm and Co., 2000), pp. 236–49.

Warminski, Andrzej, 'Introduction: Allegories of Reference', in Paul de Man, *Aesthetic Ideology*, ed. by Andrzej Warminski (Minneapolis: University of Minnesota Press, 1996), pp. 1–33.

Warren, Austin, and René Wellek, *Theory of Literature* (London: Harmondsworth, Penguin Books, 1970).

Weimann, Robert, 'Performance-Game and Representation in *Richard III*', in *Textual and Theatrical Shakespeare: Questions of Evidence*, ed. by Edward Pechter (Iowa: University of Iowa Press, 1996), pp. 66–85.

Wiggins, Martin, *Shakespeare and the Drama of His Time* (Oxford: Oxford University Press, 2000).

Willeford, William, *The Fool and His Sceptre: A Study in Clowns and Jesters and Their Audience* (Chicago: Northwestern University Press, 1969).

Zaretsky, Robert, 'The Tea Party Last Time', *The New York Times*, 2 February 2010.

Zupančič, Alenka, *The Odd One In: On Comedy* (Cambridge, MA: MIT Press, 2008).

Notes on Contributors

FABIEN ARRIBERT-NARCE is Lecturer in French at the University of Edinburgh, where his current research focuses on the reception of Japanese culture by French writers and filmmakers since 1970, and on literary and artistic responses to the Fukushima triple disaster in Japan and Europe. He is the author of *Photobiographies: pour une écriture de notation de la vie (Roland Barthes, Denis Roche, Annie Ernaux)* (Honoré Champion, 2014) and has also co-edited two multi-author volumes: *L'Autobiographie entre autres. Écrire la vie aujourd'hui* (Peter Lang, 2013) and *Réceptions de la culture japonaise en France depuis 1945. Paris-Tokyo-Paris: détours par le Japon* (Honoré Champion, 2016).

KRISTA BONELLO RUTTER GIAPPONE is Visiting Senior Lecturer in English at the University of Malta and a Research Fellow in the Centre for Critical Thought at the University of Kent, Canterbury. She is the author of a monograph entitled *The Punk Turn in Comedy: Masks of Anarchy* (Palgrave Macmillan, 2018) and has also co-edited with Fred Francis and Iain MacKenzie a volume on *Comedy and Critical Thought: Laughter as Resistance* (Rowman & Littlefield Publishers, 2018).

FUHITO ENDO is Professor of English Literature at Seikei University, Tokyo; he was Visiting Professor at University College London in 2012–3. His research specialises in the history of British psychoanalysis and its relationship with contemporary Modernist literature. He has published two monographs in Japanese on this topic; his articles in English on related themes have appeared in research journals such as *Twentieth-Century Literature*; *(a): The Journal of Culture and the Unconscious*; *Raymond Williams Studies*; and *Knots: Post-Lacanian Psychoanalysis, Literature and Film* (Routledge, 2019).

PATRICK FFRENCH is Professor of French at King's College London. His research ranges broadly across French literature, philosophy and culture of the twentieth century, with a particular focus on the interrelations of critical theory, literature and film. His publications include: *The Time of Theory: A History of "Tel Quel", 1960–83* (Clarendon Press, 1995); *The Cut: Reading Bataille's Histoire de l'œil* (Oxford University Press, 2000); *After Bataille: Sacrifice, Exposure, Community* (Legenda, 2017); *Thinking Cinema with Proust* (Legenda, 2018); *Roland Barthes and Film: Myth, Eroticism and Poetics* (Bloomsbury, 2019).

KOHEI KUWADA is Associate Professor in French and Visual Culture at the University of Tokyo. His research specialises in the work of Roland Barthes, to whom he dedicated his PhD thesis (Paris-Sorbonne University, 2009) as well as numerous books and articles published in Japanese. His research interests include modern poetry and visual art, literary criticism and post-war Japanese poetry. He has also translated several literary works and essays from French to Japanese.

KAMILA PAWLIKOWSKA currently teaches English, sociology and psychology at Rochester Independent College in Kent. Her PhD in Comparative Literature (University of Kent, 2013) was published as *Anti-Portraits: Poetics of the Face in English, Polish and Russian Literature* (Brill/Rodopi, 2015). She completed a Postdoctoral Fellowship at Seikei University, Tokyo, where she was a British Academy/Japan Society for the Promotion of Science Research Fellow and studied the perceptions of Japan in Europe. Her research interests include images of the human body and face in literature and visual arts, intercultural communication, Japanese culture and language and global education.

ANDY STAFFORD is Senior Lecturer in French at the University of Leeds. His research specialises in critical theory, especially the work of Roland Barthes; the photo-text; African and Caribbean literature, politics and historiography; the essay and other short forms. His publications include: *Roland Barthes, Phenomenon and Myth: An Intellectual Biography* (Edinburgh University Press, 1998); *Photo-texts. Contemporary French Writing of the Photographic Image* (Liverpool University Press, 2010); *Roland Barthes (Critical Lives)* (Reaktion Books, 2015).

ALEX WATSON is Associate Professor at the School of Arts and Letters in Meiji University, Tokyo. After receiving a D.Phil. in English from the University of York in 2007 and working for the University of Edinburgh and several other institutions, he arrived in Japan in March 2011. His research interests include British Romanticism, Marginalia, Paratexts, Gothic Fiction and Cinema. His major publications include *British Romanticism in Asia: The Reception, Translation, and Transformation of Romantic Literature in India and East Asia* (Palgrave Macmillan, 2019), co-edited with Laurence Williams, and *Romantic Marginality: Nation and Empire on the Borders of the Page* (Routledge, 2012). He also serves as a series co-editor for Palgrave's Asia-Pacific and Literature in English Series.

Index

Aristotle 1, 92, 96
Artaud, Antonin 7
Ayres, Philip J. 84, 89, 91, 102

Bakhtin, Mikhail 88, 98
Barthes, Roland
    Camera Lucida 2, 3, 9, 24, 28, 29, 46,
      47, 48, 53, 55, 56, 63
    Empire of Signs 2, 10–1, 16, 24, 26,
      107–16, 119–20, 122–7, 129, 131–
      45, 148–9, 151
    Michelet 11, 131, 133, 140–2, 144–
      6, 151–2
    Mythologies 24–5, 34, 38–9, 42,
      110, 123, 126–7, 130–1, 133,
      138, 143
    The Pleasure of the Text 2–5, 8, 9, 11,
      16–23, 26–34, 61–3, 65, 67–70,
      73, 111, 114, 116, 127
    *Roland Barthes by Roland
      Barthes* 47, 62, 63, 64
    S/Z 3, 5, 29–30, 44, 112, 133,
      134, 139
    'The Third Meaning' 29, 44,
      45, 46, 47
    Writing Degree Zero 24, 70, 130,
      131, 133
Bergson, Allen 84, 89, 90
Bergson, Henri 64, 88, 93, 95–6
Blake, Ann 96, 101
Blanchot, Maurice 7, 8, 66, 102
bliss *see* jouissance
Brecht, Bertolt 22, 39, 43, 45
Brooke, Nicholas 88, 96

character 4, 5, 25, 85–102
    characterisation 86, 89

cinema *see* film
Coleridge, Samuel Taylor 1
commentary 21, 29–30, 86, 102, 120,
    121, 122
contradiction 4, 7, 9, 31, 35, 67, 68, 69, 76,
    77, 90, 99, 122
Corbier, Christophe 141
Crary, Jonathan 131

De Quincey, Thomas 20, 35
death drive 67, 73, 75–6, 77, 81–2
Deleuze, Gilles 40, 45, 51–2
Derrida, Jacques 5, 8, 23
dialectics 42, 66, 77–9, 80, 131, 132, 134,
    135, 139, 141, 142–5, 147–52
    undialectical writing 136, 140, 152
drama 40, 90, 95

Ebert, Teresa 34

fatigue 9, 17, 61–6
Felman, Shoshana 71–2
fiction 5, 91, 119, 123, 124, 139
film 3, 9, 10–1, 21, 35, 37–8, 39, 40, 43–6,
    49–55, 107, 108, 111, 118–24, 126
Flaubert, Gustave 5, 6, 7, 22, 33
Foakes, Reginald A. 93, 96, 99, 102
footnotes 6, 8, 17–18, 20–2, 23–5, 32–3,
    35, 45, 126, 135
Forest, Philippe 108
Forsdick, Charles 109, 111–2, 126
Foucault, Michel 7–8, 16
Freud, Sigmund 6, 9, 22, 27, 49, 53, 67–82
Frye, Northrop 91

Genette, Gérard 8, 17–19, 23, 32, 86, 88,
    95, 99, 102

genre (literary) 10, 24, 63, 83–6, 90, 92,
    95–6, 98, 101, 103, 117, 119
Glissant, Édouard 139
Guarini, Giambattista 83

haiku 109, 114, 117, 122, 149–50, 151–2
Hegel, Georg Wilhelm Friedrich 136,
    140, 143, 147, 150, 151
Heidegger, Martin 7–8, 22
Hölderlin, Friedrich 7

identification 97, 136
image 3, 6, 9, 20, 26, 29, 30, 33, 36–57,
    63–5, 72, 107–9, 112, 114–23,
    126, 134
imaginary 1, 23, 30, 34, 36, 43, 46, 50–1,
    123–5, 144
interpretation 7, 8, 10, 17, 20, 28–32, 48,
    71, 80, 90, 95, 101, 108, 117
intertextuality 6, 19, 21, 28–30, 75, 80, 85,
    89, 102, 139
irony 40, 42–3, 74, 94–5, 126, 149
Iversen, Margaret 49–50, 67

Japan 10–1, 16, 107–27, 129, 132, 133,
    134, 138–52
Jensen, Ejner J. 101
Johnson, Samuel 15–7, 84
jouissance 2–4, 7, 9–10, 21, 27, 34, 36, 61,
    63, 65, 67–70, 73, 76–7, 79, 81–2,
    114, 116, 127

Karatani, Kōjin 80, 114, 126
Khatibi, Abdelkébir 129–30, 136
Knight, Diana 143
Kosik, Karel 132
Kydian revenge tragedy 84, 91

Lewis, Paul 83, 91–2

Macé, Marielle 139, 148
madness 8–9, 37–8, 53, 55–7

Mallarmé, Stéphane 6, 7, 22
Marker, Chris 10, 107–9, 118–27
Marston, John 10, 83–103
Mehlman, Jeffrey 9–10, 78–82
metafiction 85–7
Morin, Edgar 130, 131, 139–40
Morris, William 6

Nachtergael, Magali 131, 137
narrative 2, 18, 24, 31, 34, 52, 75, 76, 89,
    93, 115, 118, 132, 141
Natsume, Sōseki 1

paratext 6, 8, 17–21, 23, 26, 28, 29,
    31, 32, 86
Perros, Georges 151
perversity 4, 5, 8, 21, 25, 37, 45, 51, 77,
    81–2, 127
Phillips, Adam 2, 89
photography 26, 28, 31, 44–50, 52–7, 110,
    115, 118, 151
Pinguet, Maurice 107–8, 110, 115
pleasure 1–11, 16–28, 31–4, 49, 61–6,
    67–70, 73–7, 81, 83–97, 99, 101–
    3, 108–17, 125–30, 151–2
    bliss *see* jouissance
politics 2, 6–8, 10, 19, 32–4, 36, 40, 63,
    65, 77, 80–1, 115, 121, 123, 131, 136,
    143–5, 150
Pommier, René 137–9, 144
Proust, Marcel 5, 22, 23, 108, 148
psychoanalysis 5, 9, 21, 25, 27, 54,
    65, 67–76

reading 1–11, 15, 16, 17, 19–21, 25–35, 37,
    45, 57, 61–6, 67–76, 80, 81, 84–7,
    89, 91, 93, 94, 95, 99, 101, 103, 108,
    109, 112–8, 120, 123, 125, 126, 130–
    3, 137, 143, 146, 151
    projective 8, 37, 39, 44, 49,
    51, 124–5
rhetoric 31, 36, 62, 69, 77, 79, 88

Rimbaud, Arthur 7, 49
Rousseau, Jean-Jacques 1

Sartre, Jean-Paul 1, 46, 51, 64, 144
Schoenbaum, Samuel 101
semiology 9, 43, 111, 112, 116, 132, 135,
        143, 147
sexuality 2, 70, 72, 82, 89, 143
Shakespeare, William 1, 15, 16, 84, 99
signifiance 4, 5, 11, 109, 114
Simmel, Georg 35
Sontag, Susan 2, 31
Steiner, George 84
Stendhal 20, 22, 23, 33
Sterne, Laurence 1

structuralism 17–9, 24, 43, 110, 126
style 6, 18, 21, 22, 32, 33, 35, 96, 99, 121,
        132, 136, 141, 145, 148

textuality 6, 8, 10, 19, 51, 67, 70, 81
Tolstoy, Leo 22

Warminski, Andrzej 73
Weimann, Robert 87, 97
Wiggins, Martin 84, 85, 88, 94
Wilde, Oscar 1, 6
Willeford, William 97, 98

Zavarzadeh, Mas'ud 34
Zupančič, Alenka 83

European Connections

Studies in Comparative Literature, Intermediality and Aesthetics

edited by

Hugues Azérad and Marion Schmid

European Connections: Studies in Comparative Literature, Intermediality and Aesthetics is a peer-reviewed series that publishes innovative research monographs, edited volumes as well as translations of key theoretical works. The series focuses on the literary and artistic relations that have shaped and continue to shape European cultures across national, linguistic and media boundaries, leading to vibrant new forms of artistic creation and aesthetic expression. It also wishes to explore relations with non-European cultures with a view to fostering more equitable models of cultural exchange and transfer.

The series promotes comparative, intermedial and interdisciplinary approaches, whether studies of specific writers, filmmakers and artists; critical re-evaluations of historical periods (from the medieval to the ultra-contemporary) and movements; or wider theoretical reflections within the fields of comparative literature, intermediality studies and aesthetics. In light of the urgent need to revitalize the idea of Europe along new lines of thought, the series encourages research that explores the rich connections within European artistic and cultural production as well as the participation of European cultures in what the great philosopher of relation Édouard Glissant has called the *Tout-monde*. The series publishes in English, French and German.

Volume 1   S. S. Prawer: W.M. Thackeray's European Sketch Books.
A Study of Literary and Graphic Portraiture. 459 pages. 2000.
ISBN 3-906758-68-0 / US-ISBN 0-8204-5081-2

Volume 2   Patricia Zecevic: The Speaking Divine Woman. López de
Úbeda's La Pícara Justina and Goethe's Wilhelm Meister.
294 pages. 2001.
ISBN 3-906766-91-8 / US-ISBN 0-8204-5607-1

Volume 3   Mary Besemeres: Translating One's Self. Language and
Selfhood in Cross-Cultural Autobiography. 297 pages. 2002.
ISBN 3-906766-98-5 / US-ISBN 0-8204-5614-4

Volume 4   Michela Canepari-Labib: Word-Worlds. Language, Identity and
Reality in the Work of Christine Brooke-Rose. 303 pages. 2002.
ISBN 3-906758-64-8 / US-ISBN 0-8204-5080-4

Volume 5   Hugo Azérad: L'Univers constellé de Proust, Joyce et Faulkner.
Le Concept d'épiphanie dans l'esthétique du modernisme.
474 pages. 2002.
ISBN 3-906769-61-5 / US-ISBN 0-8204-5873-2

Volume 6   Berry Palmer Chevasco: Mysterymania. The Reception of
Eugène Sue in Britain 1838–1860. 284 pages. 2003.
ISBN 3-906769-78-X / US-ISBN 0-8204-5915-1

Volume 7   Sabine Schmid: 'Keeping the Sources Pure'. The Making of
George Mackay Brown. 310 pages. 2003.
ISBN 3-03910-012-2 / US-ISBN 0-8204-6281-0

Volume 8   Walter Redfern: Writing on the Move. Albert Londres and
Investigative Journalism. 266 pages. 2004.
ISBN 3-03910-157-9 / US-ISBN 0-8204-6967-X

Volume 9   Johanna Marie Buisson: Lingua Barbara or The Mystery of
the Other. Otherness and Exteriority in Modern European
Poetry. 364 pages. 2012.
ISBN 978-3-03910-057-6

Volume 10 Karl Leydecker and Nicholas White (eds): After Intimacy.
The Culture of Divorce in the West since 1789.
295 pages. 2007.
ISBN 978-3-03910-143-6

Volume 11 Patrick Crowley and Paul Hegarty: Formless. Ways In and
Out of Form. 258 pages. 2005.
ISBN 3-03910-056-4 / US-ISBN 0-8204-6297-7

Volume 12 Susan Tridgell: Understanding Our Selves. The Dangerous Art
of Biography. 234 pages. 2004.
ISBN 3-03910-166-8 / US-ISBN 0-8204-6976-9

Volume 13 Patsy Stoneman and Ana María Sánchez-Arce with Angela
Leighton (eds): European Intertexts. Women's Writing in
English in a European Context. 296 pages. 2005.
ISBN 3-03910-167-6 / US-ISBN 0-8204-6977-7

Volume 14 Daniel Hall: French and German Gothic Fiction in the Late
Eighteenth Century. 294 pages. 2005.
ISBN 3-03910-077-7 / US-ISBN 0-8204-6893-2

Volume 15 Ana Gabriela Macedo and Margarida Esteves Pereira
(eds): Identity and Cultural Translation. Writing across the
Borders of Englishness. Women's Writing in English in a
European Context. 282 pages. 2006.
ISBN 3-03910-67-2

Volume 16 Peter Wagstaff (ed.): Border Crossings. Mapping Identities in
Modern Europe. 253 pages. 2004.
ISBN 3-03910-279-6 / US-ISBN 0-8204-7206-9

Volume 17 Katharine Murphy: Re-reading Pío Baroja and English
Literature. 270 pages. 2005.
ISBN 3-03910-300-8 / US-ISBN 0-8204-7226-3

Volume 18 Elza Adamowicz (ed.): Surrealism. Crossings/Frontiers.
222 pages. 2006.
ISBN 3-03910-328-8 / US-ISBN 0-8204-7502-5

Volume 19 John Parkin and John Phillips (eds): Laughter and Power.
256 pages. 2006.
ISBN 3-03910-504-3

Volume 20 Humberto Núñez-Faraco: Borges and Dante. Echoes of a
Literary Friendship. 230 pages. 2006.
ISBN 3-03910-511-6

Volume 21 Rachael Langford (ed.): Depicting Desire. Gender, Sexuality
and the Family in Nineteenth Century Europe. Literary and
Artistic Perspectives. 280 pages. 2005.
ISBN 3-03910-321-0 / US-ISBN 0-8204-7245-X

Volume 22 Elizabeth Russell (ed.): Loving Against the Odds. Women's
Writing in English in a European Context. 222 pages. 2006.
ISBN 3-03910-732-1

Volume 23 Bruno Tribout and Ruth Whelan (eds): Narrating the Self in
Early Modern Europe. 333 pages. 2007.
ISBN 978-3-03910-740-7

Volume 24 Viola Brisolin: Power and Subjectivity in the Late Work of
Roland Barthes and Pier Paolo Pasolini. 307 pages. 2011.
ISBN 978-3-0343-0231-9

Volume 25 Gillian E. Dow (ed.): Translators, Interpreters, Mediators.
Women Writers 1700–1900. 268 pages. 2007.
ISBN 978-3-03911-055-1

Volume 26 Ramona Fotiade (ed.): The Tragic Discourse. Shestov and
Fondane's Existential Thought. 294 pages. 2006.
ISBN 3-03910-899-9

Volume 27 Annamaria Lamarra and Eleonora Federici (eds): Nations,
Traditions and Cross-Cultural Identities. Women's Writing in
English in a European Context. 185 pages. 2010.
ISBN 978-3-03911-413-9

Volume 28 Gerri Kimber: Katherine Mansfield. The View from France.
290 pages. 2008.
ISBN 978-3-03911-392-7

Volume 29 Ian R. Morrison: Leonardo Sciascia's French Authors.
179 pages. 2009.
ISBN 978-3-03911-911-0

Volume 30 Brigitte Gauthier (ed.): Viva Pinter. Harold Pinter's Spirit of
Resistance. 258 pages. 2009.
ISBN 978-3-03911-929-5

Volume 31 Hilary Brown and Gillian Dow (eds): Readers, Writers,
Salonnières. Female Networks in Europe, 1700–1900.
291 pages. 2011.
ISBN 978-3-03911-972-1

Volume 32 Nóra Séllei and June Waudby (eds): She's Leaving Home.
Women's Writing in English in a European Context.
272 pages. 2011.
ISBN 978-3-0343-0167-1

Volume 33 Lorna Collins and Elizabeth Rush (eds): Making Sense. For an
Effective Aesthetics. 250 pages. 2011.
ISBN 978-3-0343-0717-8

Volume 34   Bandy Lee and Lorna Collins (eds): Making Sense. Merging
            Theory and Practice. 280 pages. 2013.
            ISBN 978-3-0343-0763-5

Volume 35   Jane Fenoulhet: Nomadic Literature. Cees Nooteboom and
            his Writing. 257 pages. 2013.
            ISBN 978-3-0343-0729-1

Volume 36   Walter Redfern: Le Mort et le vif. Clichés/néologismes.
            428 pages. 2014.
            ISBN 978-3-0343-1754-2

Volume 37   Isabelle Chol and Jean Khalfa (eds): Les Espaces du Livre /
            Spaces of the Book. 269 pages. 2015.
            ISBN 978-3-0343-1903-4

Volume 38   Julia Effertz: Songbirds on the Literary Stage. The Woman
            Singer and her Song in French and German Prose Fiction,
            from Goethe to Berlioz. 293 pages. 2015.
            ISBN 978-3-0343-0734-5

Volume 39   Adrian Kempton: The Epistolary Muse. Women of Letters in
            England and France, 1652–1802. 374 pages. 2017.
            ISBN 978-1-78707-488-0

Volume 40   Stephen Butler: The *Fausts* of Gérard de Nerval.
            Intertextuality, Translation, Adaptation. 300 pages. 2018.
            ISBN 978-1-78874-183-5

Volume 41   Giovanni Pietro Vitali: Voices of Dissent. Interdisciplinary
            Approaches to New Italian Popular and Political Music.
            364 pages. 2020.
            ISBN 978-1-78874-204-7

Volume 42   Eva Franziska Pemmerl: Symphonie der Worte.
            Musikalisierung von Fiktion in ausgewählten Werken Irène
            Némirovskys. 270 pages. 2021.
            ISBN 978-1-78997-602-1

Volume 43   Fabien Arribert-Narce, Fuhito Endo and Kamila Pawlikowska
            (eds): The Pleasure in/of the Text. About the Joys and
            Perversities of Reading. 176 pages. 2021.
            ISBN 978-1-78997-700-4

Volume 44   Elizabeth Benjamin: Existentialist Comics. *Bande Dessinée*
            and the Art of Ethics. 2021.
            ISBN 978-1-80079-273-9